KUBLAI KHAN

KUBLAI KHAN

Kim Dramer

CHELSEA HOUSE PUBLISHERS
NEW YORK
PHILADELPHIA

Chelsea House Publishers
EDITOR-IN-CHIEF: Remmel Nunn
MANAGING EDITOR: Karyn Gullen Browne
COPY CHIEF: Juliann Barbato
PICTURE EDITOR: Adrian G. Allen
ART DIRECTOR: Maria Epes
DEPUTY COPY CHIEF: Mark Rifkin
ASSISTANT ART DIRECTOR: Loraine Machlin
MANUFACTURING MANAGER: Gerald Levine
SYSTEMS MANAGER: Rachel Vigier
PRODUCTION MANAGER: Joseph Romano
PRODUCTION COORDINATOR: Marie Claire Cebrián

World Leaders—Past & Present
SENIOR EDITOR: John W. Selfridge

Staff for KUBLAI KHAN
TEXT EDITOR: Jake Goldberg
COPY EDITOR: Richard Klin
EDITORIAL ASSISTANT: Nate Eaton
PICTURE RESEARCHERS: Michèle Brisson, Wendy Wills
DESIGNER: James Baker
COVER ILLUSTRATION: Maria Ruotolo

5 7 9 8 6 4

Library of Congress Cataloging-in-Publication Data

Dramer, Kim.
  Kublai Khan/Kim Dramer.
  p. cm.—(World leaders past & present)
  Includes bibliographical references.
  Summary: A biography of the founder of the Mongol Dynasty in
China.
  ISBN 1-55546-812-8
     0-7910-0697-2 (pbk.)
  1. Kublai Khan, 1215–94—Juvenile literature. 2. China—Kings
and rulers—Biography—Juvenile literature. [1. Kublai Khan,
1215–94. 2. Kings, queens, rulers, etc.] I. Title. II. Series.
DS752.6.K83D73   1990
950′.2′092—dc20   89–48915
[B]   CIP
[92]   AC

Contents

JOHN ADAMS

JOHN QUINCY ADAMS

KONRAD ADENAUER

ALEXANDER THE GREAT

SALVADOR ALLENDE

MARC ANTONY

CORAZON AQUINO

YASIR ARAFAT

KING ARTHUR

HAFEZ AL-ASSAD

KEMAL ATATÜRK

ATTILA

CLEMENT ATTLEE

AUGUSTUS CAESAR

MENACHEM BEGIN

DAVID BEN-GURION

OTTO VON BISMARCK

LÉON BLUM

SIMON BOLÍVAR

CESARE BORGIA

WILLY BRANDT

LEONID BREZHNEV

JULIUS CAESAR

JOHN CALVIN

JIMMY CARTER

FIDEL CASTRO

CATHERINE THE GREAT

CHARLEMAGNE

CHIANG KAI-SHEK

WINSTON CHURCHILL

GEORGES CLEMENCEAU

CLEOPATRA

CONSTANTINE THE GREAT

HERNÁN CORTÉS

OLIVER CROMWELL

GEORGES-JACQUES
DANTON

JEFFERSON DAVIS

MOSHE DAYAN

CHARLES DE GAULLE

EAMON DE VALERA

EUGENE DEBS

DENG XIAOPING

BENJAMIN DISRAELI

ALEXANDER DUBČEK

FRANÇOIS & JEAN-CLAUDE
DUVALIER

DWIGHT EISENHOWER

ELEANOR OF AQUITAINE

ELIZABETH I

FAISAL

FERDINAND & ISABELLA

FRANCISCO FRANCO

BENJAMIN FRANKLIN

FREDERICK THE GREAT

INDIRA GANDHI

MOHANDAS GANDHI

GIUSEPPE GARIBALDI

AMIN & BASHIR GEMAYEL

GENGHIS KHAN

WILLIAM GLADSTONE

MIKHAIL GORBACHEV

ULYSSES S. GRANT

ERNESTO "CHE" GUEVARA

TENZIN GYATSO

ALEXANDER HAMILTON

DAG HAMMARSKJÖLD

HENRY VIII

HENRY OF NAVARRE

PAUL VON HINDENBURG

HIROHITO

ADOLF HITLER

HO CHI MINH

KING HUSSEIN

IVAN THE TERRIBLE

ANDREW JACKSON

JAMES I

WOJCIECH JARUZELSKI

THOMAS JEFFERSON

JOAN OF ARC

POPE JOHN XXIII

POPE JOHN PAUL II

LYNDON JOHNSON

BENITO JUÁREZ

JOHN KENNEDY

ROBERT KENNEDY

JOMO KENYATTA

AYATOLLAH KHOMEINI

NIKITA KHRUSHCHEV

KIM IL SUNG

MARTIN LUTHER KING, JR.

HENRY KISSINGER

KUBLAI KHAN

LAFAYETTE

ROBERT E. LEE

VLADIMIR LENIN

ABRAHAM LINCOLN

DAVID LLOYD GEORGE

LOUIS XIV

MARTIN LUTHER

JUDAS MACCABEUS

JAMES MADISON

NELSON & WINNIE
MANDELA

MAO ZEDONG

FERDINAND MARCOS

GEORGE MARSHALL

MARY, QUEEN OF SCOTS

TOMÁŠ MASARYK

GOLDA MEIR

KLEMENS VON METTERNICH

JAMES MONROE

HOSNI MUBARAK

ROBERT MUGABE

BENITO MUSSOLINI

NAPOLÉON BONAPARTE

GAMAL ABDEL NASSER

JAWAHARLAL NEHRU

NERO

NICHOLAS II

RICHARD NIXON

KWAME NKRUMAH

DANIEL ORTEGA

MOHAMMED REZA PAHLAVI

THOMAS PAINE

CHARLES STEWART
PARNELL

PERICLES

JUAN PERÓN

PETER THE GREAT

POL POT

MUAMMAR EL-QADDAFI

RONALD REAGAN

CARDINAL RICHELIEU

MAXIMILIEN ROBESPIERRE

ELEANOR ROOSEVELT

FRANKLIN ROOSEVELT

THEODORE ROOSEVELT

ANWAR SADAT

HAILE SELASSIE

PRINCE SIHANOUK

JAN SMUTS

JOSEPH STALIN

SUKARNO

SUN YAT-SEN

TAMERLANE

MOTHER TERESA

MARGARET THATCHER

JOSIP BROZ TITO

TOUSSAINT L'OUVERTURE

LEON TROTSKY

PIERRE TRUDEAU

HARRY TRUMAN

QUEEN VICTORIA

LECH WALESA

GEORGE WASHINGTON

CHAIM WEIZMANN

WOODROW WILSON

XERXES

EMILIANO ZAPATA

ZHOU ENLAI

CHELSEA HOUSE PUBLISHERS

ON LEADERSHIP

Arthur M. Schlesinger, jr.

LEADERSHIP, it may be said, is really what makes the world go round. Love no doubt smooths the passage; but love is a private transaction between consenting adults. Leadership is a public transaction with history. The idea of leadership affirms the capacity of individuals to move, inspire, and mobilize masses of people so that they act together in pursuit of an end. Sometimes leadership serves good purposes, sometimes bad; but whether the end is benign or evil, great leaders are those men and women who leave their personal stamp on history.

Now, the very concept of leadership implies the proposition that individuals can make a difference. This proposition has never been universally accepted. From classical times to the present day, eminent thinkers have regarded individuals as no more than the agents and pawns of larger forces, whether the gods and goddesses of the ancient world or, in the modern era, race, class, nation, the dialectic, the will of the people, the spirit of the times, history itself. Against such forces, the individual dwindles into insignificance.

So contends the thesis of historical determinism. Tolstoy's great novel *War and Peace* offers a famous statement of the case. Why, Tolstoy asked, did millions of men in the Napoleonic Wars, denying their human feelings and their common sense, move back and forth across Europe slaughtering their fellows? "The war," Tolstoy answered, "was bound to happen simply because it was bound to happen." All prior history predetermined it. As for leaders, they, Tolstoy said, "are but the labels that serve to give a name to an end and, like labels, they have the least possible connection with the event." The greater the leader, "the more conspicuous the inevitability and the predestination of every act he commits." The leader, said Tolstoy, is "the slave of history."

Determinism takes many forms. Marxism is the determinism of class. Nazism the determinism of race. But the idea of men and women as the slaves of history runs athwart the deepest human instincts. Rigid determinism abolishes the idea of human freedom—

the assumption of free choice that underlies every move we make, every word we speak, every thought we think. It abolishes the idea of human responsibility, since it is manifestly unfair to reward or punish people for actions that are by definition beyond their control. No one can live consistently by any deterministic creed. The Marxist states prove this themselves by their extreme susceptibility to the cult of leadership.

More than that, history refutes the idea that individuals make no difference. In December 1931 a British politician crossing Park Avenue in New York City between 76th and 77th Streets around 10:30 P.M. looked in the wrong direction and was knocked down by an automobile—a moment, he later recalled, of a man aghast, a world aglare: "I do not understand why I was not broken like an eggshell or squashed like a gooseberry." Fourteen months later an American politician, sitting in an open car in Miami, Florida, was fired on by an assassin; the man beside him was hit. Those who believe that individuals make no difference to history might well ponder whether the next two decades would have been the same had Mario Constasino's car killed Winston Churchill in 1931 and Giuseppe Zangara's bullet killed Franklin Roosevelt in 1933. Suppose, in addition, that Adolf Hitler had been killed in the street fighting during the Munich *Putsch* of 1923 and that Lenin had died of typhus during World War I. What would the 20th century be like now?

For better or for worse, individuals do make a difference. "The notion that a people can run itself and its affairs anonymously," wrote the philosopher William James, "is now well known to be the silliest of absurdities. Mankind does nothing save through initiatives on the part of inventors, great or small, and imitation by the rest of us—these are the sole factors in human progress. Individuals of genius show the way, and set the patterns, which common people then adopt and follow."

Leadership, James suggests, means leadership in thought as well as in action. In the long run, leaders in thought may well make the greater difference to the world. But, as Woodrow Wilson once said, "Those only are leaders of men, in the general eye, who lead in action. . . . It is at their hands that new thought gets its translation into the crude language of deeds." Leaders in thought often invent in solitude and obscurity, leaving to later generations the tasks of imitation. Leaders in action—the leaders portrayed in this series—have to be effective in their own time.

And they cannot be effective by themselves. They must act in response to the rhythms of their age. Their genius must be adapted, in a phrase of William James's, "to the receptivities of the moment." Leaders are useless without followers. "There goes the mob," said the French politician hearing a clamor in the streets. "I am their leader. I must follow them." Great leaders turn the inchoate emotions of the mob to purposes of their own. They seize on the opportunities of their time, the hopes, fears, frustrations, crises, potentialities. They succeed when events have prepared the way for them, when the community is awaiting to be aroused, when they can provide the clarifying and organizing ideas. Leadership ignites the circuit between the individual and the mass and thereby alters history.

It may alter history for better or for worse. Leaders have been responsible for the most extravagant follies and most monstrous crimes that have beset suffering humanity. They have also been vital in such gains as humanity has made in individual freedom, religious and racial tolerance, social justice, and respect for human rights.

There is no sure way to tell in advance who is going to lead for good and who for evil. But a glance at the gallery of men and women in *World Leaders—Past and Present* suggests some useful tests.

One test is this: Do leaders lead by force or by persuasion? By command or by consent? Through most of history leadership was exercised by the divine right of authority. The duty of followers was to defer and to obey. "Theirs not to reason why / Theirs but to do and die." On occasion, as with the so-called enlightened despots of the 18th century in Europe, absolutist leadership was animated by humane purposes. More often, absolutism nourished the passion for domination, land, gold, and conquest and resulted in tyranny.

The great revolution of modern times has been the revolution of equality. The idea that all people should be equal in their legal condition has undermined the old structure of authority, hierarchy, and deference. The revolution of equality has had two contrary effects on the nature of leadership. For equality, as Alexis de Tocqueville pointed out in his great study *Democracy in America*, might mean equality in servitude as well as equality in freedom.

"I know of only two methods of establishing equality in the political world," Tocqueville wrote. "Rights must be given to every citizen, or none at all to anyone . . . save one, who is the master of all." There was no middle ground "between the sovereignty of all and the absolute power of one man." In his astonishing prediction of 20th-century totalitarian dictatorship, Tocqueville explained how the revolution of equality could lead to the *"Führerprinzip"* and more terrible absolutism than the world had ever known.

But when rights are given to every citizen and the sovereignty of all is established, the problem of leadership takes a new form, becomes more exacting than ever before. It is easy to issue commands and enforce them by the rope and the stake, the concentration camp and the *gulag.* It is much harder to use argument and achievement to overcome opposition and win consent. The Founding Fathers of the United States understood the difficulty. They believed that history had given them the opportunity to decide, as Alexander Hamilton wrote in the first Federalist Paper, whether men are indeed capable of basing government on "reflection and choice, or whether they are forever destined to depend . . . on accident and force."

Government by reflection and choice called for a new style of leadership and a new quality of followership. It required leaders to be responsive to popular concerns, and it required followers to be active and informed participants in the process. Democracy does not eliminate emotion from politics; sometimes it fosters demagoguery; but it is confident that, as the greatest of democratic leaders put it, you cannot fool all of the people all of the time. It measures leadership by results and retires those who overreach or falter or fail.

It is true that in the long run despots are measured by results too. But they can postpone the day of judgment, sometimes indefinitely, and in the meantime they can do infinite harm. It is also true that democracy is no guarantee of virtue and intelligence in government, for the voice of the people is not necessarily the voice of God. But democracy, by assuring the right of opposition, offers built-in resistance to the evils inherent in absolutism. As the theologian Reinhold Niebuhr summed it up, "Man's capacity for justice makes democracy possible, but man's inclination to injustice makes democracy necessary."

A second test for leadership is the end for which power is sought. When leaders have as their goal the supremacy of a master race or the promotion of totalitarian revolution or the acquisition and exploitation of colonies or the protection of greed and privilege or the preservation of personal power, it is likely that their leadership will do little to advance the cause of humanity. When their goal is the abolition of slavery, the liberation of women, the enlargement of opportunity for the poor and powerless, the extension of equal rights to racial minorities, the defense of the freedoms of expression and opposition, it is likely that their leadership will increase the sum of human liberty and welfare.

Leaders have done great harm to the world. They have also conferred great benefits. You will find both sorts in this series. Even "good" leaders must be regarded with a certain wariness. Leaders are not demigods; they put on their trousers one leg after another just like ordinary mortals. No leader is infallible, and every leader needs to be reminded of this at regular intervals. Irreverence irritates leaders but is their salvation. Unquestioning submission corrupts leaders and demeans followers. Making a cult of a leader is always a mistake. Fortunately hero worship generates its own antidote. "Every hero," said Emerson, "becomes a bore at last."

The signal benefit the great leaders confer is to embolden the rest of us to live according to our own best selves, to be active, insistent, and resolute in affirming our own sense of things. For great leaders attest to the reality of human freedom against the supposed inevitabilities of history. And they attest to the wisdom and power that may lie within the most unlikely of us, which is why Abraham Lincoln remains the supreme example of great leadership. A great leader, said Emerson, exhibits new possibilities to all humanity. "We feed on genius. . . . Great men exist that there may be greater men."

Great leaders, in short, justify themselves by emancipating and empowering their followers. So humanity struggles to master its destiny, remembering with Alexis de Tocqueville: "It is true that around every man a fatal circle is traced beyond which he cannot pass; but within the wide verge of that circle he is powerful and free; as it is with man, so with communities."

1

Conquerors from the Steppes

In the ninth moon of the year 1224, Genghis, Khan of Khans, commanded the Great Hunt to begin. Astride his Mongol pony, Kublai, the royal prince, watched as soldiers laid out the starting line for the Great Hunt. The line stretched for 80 miles across the plains of central Asia, its length marked by silk banners to show the assembly point for each army unit. Riders were dispatched to mark the finishing point hundreds of miles ahead. Horns and drums signaled the start, and the Mongol troops rode forward in a single line, driving all game before them.

Kublai was now nine summers old. He was small for his age, with a swarthy complexion and piercing black eyes. Now he was ready to prove that he had inherited the courage and cunning of his grandfather Genghis, Khan of Khans. A man who proved himself in the Great Hunt could win an exalted position in the Khan's army. The young prince, who wished to be a great warrior on the battlefield of the Mongols and cover himself with blood and glory, knew this well and was eager to demonstrate his prowess with bow and arrow on the field. He intended to prove himself worthy of the honor of joining the Mongol troops.

Under the leadership of Genghis Khan . . . the Mongols burst upon the rest of Asia.
—MORRIS ROSSABI
American historian

Mongol warriors slay deer, hare, and other more fanciful beasts in this depiction of a Great Hunt. In the upper right corner of the picture, a horseman is about to release his trained falcon. On the left another hunter wields a mace.

The lonely, windswept grasslands of Mongolia have not changed their appearance in 800 years, and neither have the nomadic tribes that inhabit them. The tribes still depend heavily upon horses and live in circular felt tents known as *yurts*.

Weeks went by as the disciplined horsemen continued their march, herding the wild animals before them. At last, soldiers in the wings of the line advanced rapidly to the finishing point and rode toward each other, totally encircling the game. During the drive it was forbidden to make a kill. There would be time for that later. Rather, the objective was to prevent the game from breaking through the circle of horsemen. If any horseman allowed even a single small animal to escape, he and his officer would likely be punished severely.

The smallest of animals was relentlessly herded forward, the ring of soldiers contracting around the terrified animals as the soldiers maneuvered to prevent any escape. As the circle grew smaller and smaller, the swiftest and cleverest animals, such as wolves, tested the soldiers' skill.

During the march, Kublai learned to sleep only every other day. Half the soldiers kept watch each night to make sure no animals broke through the line; the other half slept around the campfires, fully clothed and ready for action at any moment. Kublai was part of a huge human amphitheater of Mongol soldiers, with thousands of terrified animals trapped in its arena.

At dawn on the final day of the Great Hunt, Kublai watched as Genghis rode first into the arena. With much ceremony, the Great Khan loosed an arrow to begin the killing. Many would show enormous courage that day. Mounted men used bow and arrow to slay the beasts. Others, on foot, killed great boars with their swords. As Mongol history has it, the fiercest of the warriors took on tigers with their bare hands. Genghis watched closely as the killing took place. Silently he noted the skill of one man, the recklessness of another, the bravery of a third. The ground ran red with blood, and the air was filled with the screams of dying animals and wounded men.

Kublai fitted an arrow in his bow and let it fly. It found its mark, killing a large hare. He urged his pony forward into the arena to claim his prize. Tonight he would offer the animal to his grandfather, the Great Khan.

The killing continued all day until the sun began to set. By tradition, the young princes of the blood and the honored old warriors knelt before their Khan. In one voice they begged the Khan to spare the lives of the remaining animals. The horns and drums rang out again. The Great Hunt was over.

Kublai knelt once more before his grandfather. He held his trophy in both hands, placing it at the Great Khan's feet. Genghis accepted the hare from his grandson. It was a fine kill. The boy's arrow had pierced the creature through the eye, killing it cleanly.

The Great Khan himself performed Kublai's baptism of the hunt. Drawing his jeweled dagger from his belt, Genghis slit open the belly of the hare. He cut off a piece of flesh and fat. Seizing Kublai's hand in his battle-hardened grasp, Genghis wrapped the boy's middle finger in the warm flesh, praying to the Great Heaven to always grant his grandson rich bags of game and success over his enemies. Then he nicked Kublai's finger with his knife, catching the blood in a bowl and mingling it with wine and meat. Kublai drank from the bowl and ate the meat seasoned with his own blood. The ritual was complete. Kublai had taken the first step toward becoming a Mongol warrior.

It had been by Genghis Khan's decree that the Great Hunt was introduced as part of Mongol military training. It gave soldiers a chance to prove their

A modern Mongolian shepherd boy tends his sheep. Flocks of animals were the only wealth known to the ancient Mongol clans before they invaded other lands. A storm, drought, or raiding party from a rival clan could easily render the richest family destitute.

The Mongols took the wool from their sheep and with continual wetting and pressing turned it into a thick, dense felt — both warm and windproof — that was the ideal material for their tents.

bravery in the presence of the Great Khan. More importantly, it was a military exercise designed to inspire team spirit and to teach the legions of Mongol horsemen, the finest light cavalry of their time, how to move in large, terrifying formations. In times of peace, the Great Hunt could last up to three months. The disciplined maneuvers and rigid adherence to commands caused the troops to think and act like one man. Such *esprit de corps* was vital for highly mobile mounted troops like the Mongol army.

Now the Great Khan sat on his throne of sacred white horse skins. It was time for the feasting to begin. Around the campfires men ate of the game they had killed that day, roasting the animals whole and cutting off chunks of meat with their daggers. They downed cup after cup of a strong liquor called *koumiss*, made from the fermented milk of their mares. Those who had won honor were brought before the Great Khan and rewarded.

The year had been a good one. The Mongol army had conquered the central Asian kingdom of Khwaresmia. Genghis's army had left 15 million dead and a devastated land, but his people had been enriched by booty and slaves.

Now it was time to return to the Mongolian Plateau and the ancient ways of the people. For it was from their land and their traditional way of life that the Mongols drew their strength.

The Mongol homeland was centered in the stretch of country between the Onon and Kerulen rivers on the eastern Mongolian Plateau. It was there, in 1206, that the Mongols bestowed upon the warrior named Temüjin the title of Khan, meaning chieftain or king. His first name, Genghis, meant all the seas encompassed by the world-girdling ocean.

The vast steppes of the Mongolian Plateau are harsh and barren. From the open sky above the steppes, little rain falls, and no rivers flow out to the sea. The dry land spreads out endlessly under the open sky. Mile upon mile of arid land is punctuated by only the hardiest of plants, their deep roots probing the earth for sustenance.

So, too, the Mongols of Inner Asia had been forced to scratch a living from the hostile earth. Like the hardy plants, the population of the steppes was sparse and scattered. There were no farms to coax grain from the earth, no cities to engage in commerce and trade. Yet the roots of the Mongol people in this barren land were deep and strong. These very

Mongol women display their family wealth and status with richly ornamented, jewel-studded headdresses and elaborately designed robes of pure silk.

same harsh conditions made the Mongol warrior the most self-reliant and fiercest soldier in the world.

The Mongols lived a nomadic life in felt tents called *yurts* and sustained themselves by raising animals, particularly horses and sheep. They lived a nomadic life, moving their flocks from the open plains of summer to spend the harsh winter in the sheltered mountain valleys in a seasonal migration. From their flocks Mongols obtained skins for their clothing and felt for their dwellings. The felt was made by pounding animal fur into a strong, dense cloth to keep out the bitter wind that swept unchecked across the treeless steppes. The rounded yurts were dismantled and carried across the Mongolian Plateau when the seasonal migration came, and the camp moved in search of better pasture. Sheep supplied mutton, milk, and cheese — the staples of the Mongols' diet. Fires for warmth and cooking were fueled by animal dung gathered by the Mongol women.

Mounted on sturdy horses, the Mongol men managed the flocks and hunted game. Children were hardened by long hours in the saddle. Women as well as men were taught to ride, and like their husbands, they were excellent bow hunters. Theirs was

Mongolian youngsters today learn to ride almost as soon as they can walk. So it must have been with the young Kublai, performing feats of horsemanship before his proud grandfather, Genghis the Conqueror, during hunts and competitions.

The Mongolian pony is small, as horses go, but known for its strength and endurance. Trained riders could make them race, stop, and turn with the precision of infantry units but much faster. In massed squadrons they must have presented a sight that no ancient army had seen before.

a harsh existence, and Mongol horsemen became independent and self-reliant at an early age.

Like all Mongol boys, Kublai learned to ride while very young. His first toy was a small bow and arrows, which he shot at rabbits and small game on the steppes. The hunting skills Kublai developed as a child helped prepare him for the military training he received later in life.

Although the Mongol nomads were basically self-sufficient, they were not isolated from commercial centers. The summer pastures were just north of the Great Wall that protected the kingdom of China and its rich, cultivated farmland. The pastoral Mongols traded with the farmers to obtain grain, tea, textiles, and metal with which to make weapons. Their precarious nomadic existence gave them an incentive to develop military prowess and prey upon their neighbors. One's survival depended on one's skills in horsemanship and archery. A Mongol's status in the clan and his success in providing for his family depended on his ability as a warrior and his cunning in raids.

Wealth, measured in horses and flocks, was a precarious asset. A harsh winter could kill the animals, and the climate of the steppes was unpredictable. In late winter, Mongols particularly feared the *jud*, a brief warm spell that melted the snow and was followed by a cold wave that formed a crust of ice over the ground. Grazing animals were unable to penetrate the ice layer to reach forage below. The consequences were devastating. With no stores of fodder, the animals starved to death. In the thaw that followed, the steppes were littered with their carcasses.

Equally feared were the thunderstorms that struck without warning. The dry air crackled with lightning that caused many deaths and terrified the Mongols and their animals. The ground could not absorb the sudden downpour, and flooding occurred frequently. The rushing waters washed away the yurts, drowning men and entire flocks. Disease and wolves could rob a man of his holdings, and a rival clan might launch a raiding party to take by force what they needed to survive.

Besides livestock and horses, raiders sought human plunder. They took slaves to work in their camps, and more importantly, they sought women, for Mongol tradition forbade them from marrying within their own clan.

Mongol society was a patriarchal one in which men had as many wives as they wished. Each wife had to be provided with her own yurt, but only one woman could be the chief wife; her male children would inherit all the clan's wealth upon the death of the father. Each clan formed its own independent *ordu*, the Mongol word for camp. Mongol women performed the household chores that sustained life in the ordu and also took on numerous other responsibilities when the men went out on raiding parties. When the men returned, the women shared equally in the spoils. Mongol society was ordered by strict rules; loyalties and duties were clearly established and strictly enforced.

The principle weapon of the Mongol warrior was the longbow. With a range of 200 yards, it could wreak havoc on the enemy without subjecting the archer to any danger. In an age of swords, pikes, and spears, such a long-range weapon was revolutionary.

Genghis Khan holds court before his sons, client princes, and visiting ambassadors. His elaborate throne shows how the Mongols in their conquests were learning to use the symbols of wealth and power and were slowly turning from their nomadic ways.

Mounted on swift horses, the Mongols swooped down upon their enemies and loosed their deadly arrows. Just as quickly, they disappeared into the steppes, retreating with their plunder back to the yurts. The Mongol clan system rewarded those who displayed military prowess during these raids. Chieftains were selected on the basis of their demonstrated success in hunting and combat. Strength and cunning were rewarded, and old or weak chiefs were replaced.

At first, the Mongols only attacked each other's camps. When one clan conquered another, the victors assimilated the losers into their own clan. The defeated clan took on the name of the victorious one. Shamans, the religious men and storytellers, would then fabricate legends saying that the clans were really descended from two brothers or related in some special way in the distant past. In this way the old feuds were buried, and some clans grew larger and more powerful than others.

Genghis's father had been a member of the Borjigin clan. The origin of this clan was recited in the legends of the shamans: In the northern forests there roamed a great blue-gray wolf. By the shores of Lake Baikal, he took as his consort a tawny doe. The pair then traveled south and settled near the Kentey Range, where the Onon River rises at the foot of a mountain called Burkan-Kaldun. From the union of the wolf and the doe, the Mongols sprang. The Borjigin clan claimed direct descent from the wolf and the doe.

There had been incessant bloodshed among the tribes of the Mongolian Plateau until Genghis united the clans. Genghis believed he had a divine mission sanctioned by the god the Mongols worshiped as Möngke Tenggeri. Heaven itself had decreed that he should rule over all those who lived in yurts.

Under Genghis, the larger clans swallowed the smaller ones, and Mongol raiding parties grew into armies. Attacks grew more frequent and the spoils larger. Eventually, the attacks became carefully planned, full-scale campaigns. Genghis organized the tribes of Mongolia into an unstoppable, highly mobile military machine. He succeeded in fulfilling the dream of his ancestral Borjigin clan: to "bind the arrows into a bundle" so that the Mongols would be united and strong.

Genghis Khan's army ultimately forged the largest empire *ever* to exist upon the face of the earth up to the 13th century. Yet Genghis's conquest was still not finished. He would leave that for his sons, and his sons' sons.

> *All his natural talent would not have got him very far . . . if he had not been born at a propitious time and in just the right geographical location.*
> —OWEN LATTIMORE
> American Orientalist, on
> Genghis Khan

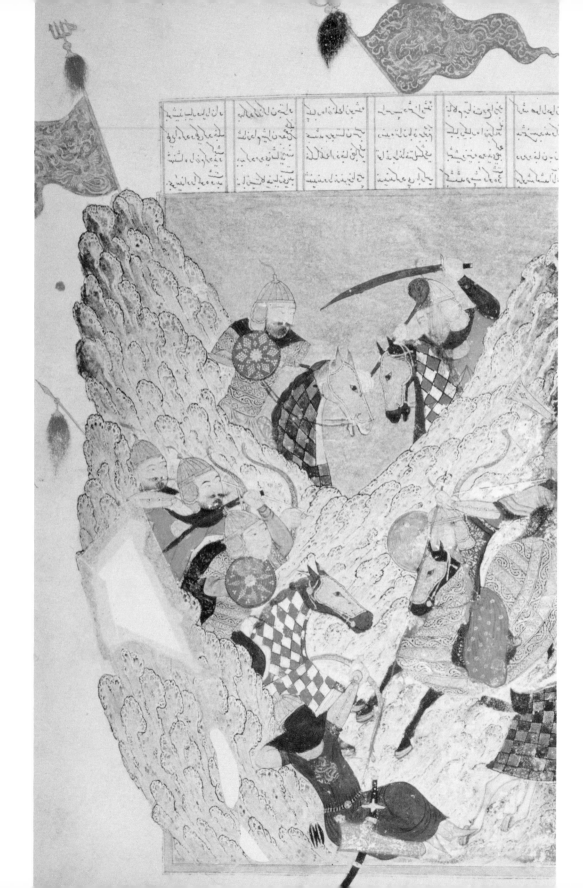

2

The Warrior Emerges

Kublai was born in 1215, the year that the Great Khan conquered the city of Beijing in China, sacking the town and putting to the torch its beautiful palaces, wide streets, and lovely gardens.

Kublai's mother, Sorghaghtani Beki, had herself been part of the human plunder Genghis had acquired during the unification wars he waged on the Mongolian Plateau. She was the niece of Ong Khan, ruler of the Kereyid tribe. Genghis subjugated the Kereyids and offered Sorghaghtani Beki in marriage to his own youngest son, Tolui.

Genghis had chosen well for Tolui: Sorghaghtani Beki was both beautiful and intelligent. All who met her remarked on her abilities, saying she towered among all the women in the world. "If I were to see a race of women like this," wrote one 13th-century poet, "I should say that the race of women was far superior to that of men!"

[Kublai Khan] won the lordship by his own valour and good sense; his kinsfolk and brothers tried to debar him from it, but by his great prowess he won it. And you must know that it was properly his by right.
—MARCO POLO
Venetian traveler

This painting depicts fierce fighting between Mongolian cavalry and the Chinese Sung armies somewhere in the mountains of northern China during the campaigns of Genghis Khan, when Kublai was still just a princely servant of his grandfather's. The artist has shown the importance of the mounted archer in Mongol battle strategy.

Sorghaghtani Beki was to bear her husband four sons: Mangu, Kublai, Hülegü, and Arigböge. She and her husband were often separated, for Tolui always accompanied his father to war. He commanded one of the main detachments of Genghis Khan's army during the conquest of Central Asia. Tolui relished combat and the wild Mongol celebrations of feasting and drinking that followed victory. He especially loved to drink great quantities of koumiss.

After the death of Genghis in 1227, Tolui's brother, Ögödei, was proclaimed Great Khan. Tolui continued to wage war in the service of his brother.

Like all Mongol women, Sorghaghtani Beki assumed total responsibility for managing the family estates while her husband was away. Her main concern was to raise her four sons. She had lofty ambitions for the young princes of the house of Tolui. Her four sons learned to ride and shoot; to love the hunt and the glory of conquest. Their mother engaged a Uighur tutor named Tolochu to teach them to read and write the new Mongol written language, adapted from the Uighur Turkish script in 1204 by one of Genghis Khan's captive scholars. She also encouraged her sons to excel in the athletic contests for young boys held at Mongol celebrations.

In 1231, when Tolui died, Kublai was 16 years old. Fact and fiction are difficult to distinguish in tales told about Tolui's death. Mongol histories portray his passing as an act of valor and sacrifice in the service of his brother, the Great Khan Ögödei. Ögödei had been stricken with an evil malady. In the shaman's yurt, he lay gasping as his end approached. Tolui, beside himself with grief, rushed into the yurt and screamed, "Take me instead of Ögödei." Tolui fell to the floor, stricken. Shortly thereafter, the Great Khan rose from his bed. He had been cured. But Tolui died the next day, having given his life for his brother.

Other historians, less concerned with creating heroic legends, say that koumiss brought about Tolui's death. He had become too fond of his frequent and full cups of the strong drink, and the overindulgence had finally killed him.

A portrait of Ögödei, who served as Great Khan after the death of Genghis. His son Güyük succeeded him for a brief period, but a power struggle between the clans soon elevated Mangu, Kublai's brother, to the throne.

Ögödei sought to marry the widowed Sorghagh-tani Beki to his son Güyük, the child of his chief wife, Töregene. The union between aunt and nephew would unite two princely families and assure an orderly succession for the Great Khanate.

The precarious life of the Mongol nomad made it imperative to ensure that widows and children would be taken care of. A male relative from a man's clan usually married his widow and took her children under his protection. The family estate thus remained intact, and the family bond strengthened.

Sorghaghtani Beki courteously refused Ögödei's offer, citing her duty to Tolui's sons. She thought only of raising her children until they reached manhood and independence. The widow now requested an appanage, or land grant, that would enable her to govern and collect tax revenues. Ögödei granted her a district in northern China called Chen-ting, taken from the conquered territory added to the Mongol empire.

Now, with a province of her own to govern, Sorgh-aghtani Beki began the education of her sons in the art of administration and politics. Sorghaghtani

An old Mongolian shepherd drinks *koumiss*, the traditional drink made from fermented mare's milk, as his granddaughter watches. In ancient cultures with poor sanitary conditions, drinking an alcoholic beverage was probably safer than drinking water.

Beki was a Christian of the Nestorian sect. In Chen-ting, however, she patronized Buddhism and Taoism as well, gaining the support of her new subjects. She gave funds to build mosques and seminaries for Moslem students, yet remained faithful to her Nestorian Christian religion.

In order to govern Chen-ting effectively, Sorghaghtani Beki had to formulate new policies to govern a population of settled farmers. Her fairness and liberality resulted in increased tax revenues. She put her new wealth to good use, maneuvering the house of Tolui into a position to inherit the Great Khanate. She provided generous gifts to the Mongol nobility and rewarded all their envoys and messengers richly. Aware that her situation was dependent on the grace of the Great Khan, she strictly observed traditional Mongol customs and practices and was always deferential to Ögödei.

In 1236, Ögödei offered an appanage in northern China to Kublai himself. The district of Hsing-chou was a farming region with some 10,000 households. It was the first domain that Kublai ruled.

Kublai governed as an absentee ruler, spending most of his time on the steppes of Mongolia, close to his uncle, the Great Khan. He was not able to keep an eye on the behavior of his appointed officials, mostly Mongols, who burdened the farmers of

Hsing-chou with their excessive greed. Kublai's overseers crushed the farmers with demands of cor-vée labor — service that subjects were required to render to their sovereign without compensation. Tax collectors squeezed the farmers of Hsing-chou severely. Kublai's inattention to the problems of governing would cause him difficulties again, much later, when an entire empire was at stake.

The oppressed farmers fled the district and re-settled in areas that were not under Mongol domi-nation. By the time Kublai was made aware of the situation, many of the original households of his appanage had abandoned their farms. Kublai quickly replaced his Mongol officials with local administrators, men who better understood the patterns and rhythms of agricultural life. Following his mother's example in Chen-ting, Kublai adopted a code of laws and tax policies more consistent with the agrarian way of life in his district.

The settled agricultural society of China, built around the cultivation of rice, was a new experience for the Mongols, who were used to thinking of wealth as whatever they could carry away in raids. Kublai's experience in managing his lands in northern China broadened his understanding of this new way of producing wealth.

Kublai's new policies put an end to the exodus of farmers from Hsing-chou. Those who had left began to return to their homes. The region was stabilized once again, and Kublai's rule was made secure. Sorghaghtani Beki's lessons had been learned well.

Now she searched among the maidens for wives to marry her sons. If the men of the house of Tolui were to be conquerors of great empires, they would need to have capable women back home ruling during their absence.

During Kublai's life, he was to have four main wives, each with her own ordu. Under each main wife were a number of subordinate wives and concubines. Little is known of Kublai's first main wife, Tegülün, and her life in the first ordu.

In 1240, Kublai married his second wife, Chabi, the daughter of Alchi Noyan. Chabi aspired to be the wife of a great chieftain, not simply the wife of a minor prince. She was the ideal helpmate for Kublai, and like Sorghaghtani Beki, Chabi became an influential adviser to her husband.

Whereas Sorghaghtani Beki was a devout Nestorian Christian, Chabi was an ardent Buddhist. She was especially attracted to Tibetan Buddhism and gave her first son the Tibetan name Dorji. She donated some of her jewelry to Buddhist monasteries when Kublai invited Buddhist monks to Hsing-chou. Of all the religions of Asia, Buddhism would always occupy a privileged position in Kublai's realm, but he was flexible and tolerant of other religions and never really adopted a single set of beliefs for himself.

Genghis had not established a system of precise and orderly succession to the Khanate. When a Great Khan died, a *khuriltai* was convened. This was a meeting of the most prominent Mongol nobles, who elected a new Great Khan by choosing the strongest and most able from among Genghis Khan's heirs. Only Genghis's direct descendants, known collectively as the Golden Kin, could rule the Mongol empire and its vassal states.

Events the next year turned in favor of the house of Tolui. Sorghaghtani Beki and Chabi watched as the clan advanced one step closer to the Great Khan-

This painting depicts a Mongol *khuriltai* in session. These councils of leading nobles were convened to select a new Great Khan upon the death of the previous ruler. Because the throne was not automatically passed on to the oldest son, plots and intrigues arose among the most powerful clans.

ate. In 1241, Ögödei, the Great Khan, died. Ögödei had favored his grandson Shiremün as his successor. But Ögödei's chief wife, Töregene, used her position to advance her own son, Güyük, toward the throne. Güyük, whom Ögödei had earlier proposed as a husband for the widowed Sorghaghtani Beki, was away on a military campaign in the West. His mother had herself been appointed regent in his absence. When Güyük returned to the Mongol homeland in 1246, Töregene installed her son on the sacred white horse-skin throne as Great Khan.

Töregene's administration during her regency had been corrupt and inefficient. Her scheming had made many enemies. At the same time, Sorghaghtani Beki had secretly advanced her plans for the house of Tolui. She sought allies among the Mongol nobility who would convene the khuriltai that elected the next Great Khan. Her greatest ally was the Mongol chieftain Batu, a grandson of Genghis Khan's and Sorghaghtani Beki's nephew.

A deep hatred had developed between Batu and Güyük during the western campaign. In 1247, Güyük, now installed as Great Khan, decided to launch a surprise attack against Batu. When Sorghaghtani Beki learned of his plans, she secretly warned Batu. To be discovered meant death, but she was willing to risk even that in her quest for the Great Khanate. She was fortunate. Güyük died en route to the attack, another Mongol leader killed by the excessive consumption of koumiss. Sorghaghtani Beki's gamble had paid off.

Batu, Sorghaghtani Beki, and her four sons now formed a powerful alliance. In 1251, they convened

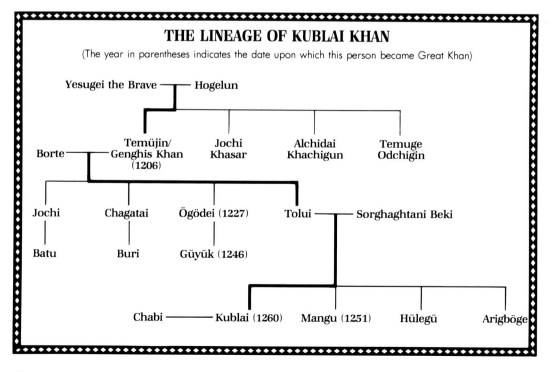

THE LINEAGE OF KUBLAI KHAN

(The year in parentheses indicates the date upon which this person became Great Khan)

A section of the Great Wall running through the mountainous terrain of northern China. Perhaps the greatest feat of construction ever accomplished, the wall was nevertheless useless in keeping out the Mongol invaders.

a khuriltai in central Asia at which Mangu, Kublai's elder brother, was proclaimed Great Khan. Sorgh-aghtani Beki had achieved her goal. The house of Tolui now sat on the throne of sacred white horse skins. She enjoyed her victory only briefly. In 1252 she died, and her grieving sons erected a tablet in her memory in her appanage of Chen-ting.

Mangu's ascension to the throne angered the house of Ögödei. They maintained that since the khuriltai had been held in central Asia rather than in the Mongols' traditional homeland, Mangu's claim was illegitimate. Güyük's widow, Oghul Ghaimish, sought to overthrow the house of Tolui by armed rebellion. Mangu crushed her opposition quickly, executing those who had opposed him.

Kublai had been born at the start of the Mongol expansion and had grown to manhood as the Mongol armies spread far to the north and west. Now, with the throne secure, Mangu Khan set out with Kublai to pacify the lands to the east and south. Kublai was to lead one of Mangu's armies in the final conquest of China.

Northern China had already been subdued as the Mongols attacked from the north, breaching the Great Wall. They had driven the court of the Chinese

This ancient wood-block print shows Mongol horsemen parading before the Great Wall as the Chinese defenders look on warily. The mobility of the Mongol cavalry overwhelmed Chinese armies encountered in the field, but to conquer the cities the Mongols had to learn siege tactics.

Sung emperor from his capital at Kaifeng. The Sung emperor reestablished his court at Lin-an, today's Hangchow, south of the Yangtze River. It was the largest city in the world at that time and protected by a strong defense.

In 1258, Kublai and Mangu set off for China. First they visited one of Genghis's old palaces, where they performed ritual sacrifices to ensure the Mongol army's success. The Mongol troops that sought to conquer southern China numbered in the hundreds of thousands and were divided into two armies. Mangu would head one army and Kublai another.

Mangu prepared meticulously for the battle. His plan was to advance his troops in a pincer movement against the Sung army. But Mangu's military advisers expressed their doubts about victory. Natural conditions favored the Sung troops. The Mongols were used to the cool, dry climate of their homeland, and the weather in southern China was hot and humid. There was little fodder for horses, and there were diseases in the area that might sicken the Mongol warriors.

The strength of the Mongol army was its highly mobile cavalry, which could not move swiftly in the hilly terrain of southern China, crisscrossed as it was by rivers, canals, and lakes. The Mongols would have to use their infantry and lay siege to the principal Sung cities.

Mangu angrily replied to his advisers that he was determined to finish the conquest his ancestors had started. He would seek a quick victory for the Mongol army that would spare his men the suffering of a long campaign. Kublai's troops were to pin down the Sung forces along the middle reaches of the Yangtze River. Mangu himself would cross the river and attack the Sung army from the west.

The Chinese had good reason to hate and fear the Mongols, for they were frequently tyrannized by them.
—R. CROSBIE-WESTON
American historian

Mangu met with some initial success, but progress was slow and costly. In 1259, Mangu held a banquet for his generals. After feasting and drinking, they expressed their concern again over the difficulties of fighting in a land so different from the vast, open plains of the Mongol homeland. They were especially concerned about the number of men who had succumbed to illness. But Mangu was determined to complete his conquest.

In August of that year, as Mangu led his troops in an attack against the Sung city of Ho-chou, he fell from his horse. Sung sources say he was wounded in battle and died soon after. The Mongols claim the warrior was felled by dysentery.

In 1260, the Mongol army in China proclaimed Kublai as Mangu's successor. The conquest of China would be completed by Kublai, the Great Khan.

3

The Great Khan

One of Kublai's first acts upon becoming Great Khan was to move the Mongol capital from Karakorum on the Mongolian Plateau to Beijing in northern China. This was the city his grandfather Genghis had conquered and destroyed in 1215, the year of Kublai's birth. Kublai called the city Ta-tu, or the great capital.

Kublai's younger brother, Arigböge, had remained in Mongolia to guard the ancestral homeland during the military expedition of his older brothers, Kublai and Mangu, in south China. Arigböge was the fourth and youngest son of Sorghaghtani Beki and Tolui. His Mongolian nickname was the Little One. One month after Kublai's election to the white horse-skin throne, Arigböge challenged Kublai's election as Great Khan. He had himself proclaimed Great Khan in Karakorum and launched a series of raids against Kublai's troops in north China.

Support for the Little One grew. Many conservative Mongol nobles were angered that the khuriltai that had elected Kublai had been assembled in the north Chinese city of Shang-tu. They were outraged at the relocation of the capital outside the Mongol homeland.

The Great Khan is the wisest man and the ablest in all respects, the best rule of subjects and of empire and the man of the highest character of all that have ever been in the whole history of the Tartars.
—MARCO POLO
Venetian traveler, on Kublai Khan

A portrait of Kublai Khan, the first Mongol chieftain to conquer and rule all of China. In order to do so effectively, he had to abandon many traditional Mongol ways, which angered other Mongol nobles and set them against his rule.

Now Kublai had to battle for his throne against his younger brother. Arigböge's advisers first sought to defeat Kublai by deceit and treachery. They counseled Arigböge to send messengers to Kublai summoning him north to the Mongolian Plateau where Arigböge might seize and kill him. In order to mourn for Mangu Khan, Arigböge had written, it was necessary that Kublai and all the other princes come north.

Kublai's wife Chabi, sensing a trick, tried to stall Arigböge's collaborators and sent a secret message to Kublai urging him to return to Mongolia and defend his throne. Without Chabi's timely warning, Kublai's position would have been severely weakened.

Kublai immediately turned his army around and set off for Mongolia to protect his claim, leaving only a small force to guard his conquests in China. The Sung army immediately converged on the Mongol

A Persian depiction of a battle between rival Mongol factions. Throughout his reign, Kublai was plagued by challenges to his rule from his blood relations. The rebellion of Arigböge was one of the most serious.

rear guard and reoccupied their lost lands. They strengthened their resolve not to deal with the barbarians, a decision they would pay for dearly in the future.

Kublai's strategy for dealing with Arigböge was simple: He would use the plentiful resources available in agrarian north China and deny them to Arigböge's troops on the Mongolian steppes by blocking the supply routes to Karakorum. At Karakorum, the harsh land could not support Arigböge's army. He had to transport most of the food and supplies over long distances. Kublai's troops, however, were well supplied in their north China base. Both armies set up their winter camps and waited for the spring before taking further action.

Once again, Arigböge sent a false message to Kublai, trying to lure him into a trap. Kublai's younger brother claimed to have transgressed out of ignorance and promised never again to deviate from Kublai's commands. But Kublai remembered his brother's first entreaty and prepared for battle. He assembled an army of 50,000 men and laid in stores and equipment. In 1261, the armies of the two brothers clashed. Arigböge's defeated troops retreated, but he continued his fight and refused to surrender.

Great Heaven itself seemed to turn against Arigböge. One day, the legends say, as the Little One sat feasting and drinking koumiss, a whirlwind suddenly sprang up and ripped the pegs of his audience tent from the earth. The supporting poles of the tent were broken, and several people were killed. It was a bad omen, predicting the decline of his fortune. Many of Arigböge's followers abandoned him. In truth, though, the harsh conditions of the Mongol homeland and Kublai's blockade had done him in. The winter of 1263 was especially bitter. There was starvation in Arigböge's camp when supplies could not get through.

Arigböge realized that he would have to surrender. He traveled to Kublai's camp at Shang-tu, where Kublai had established his summer capital. He and his generals entered Kublai's audience tent and fell to their knees weeping before the Great Khan. Ku-

They eat the flesh of no matter what animal, even dogs and swine. They open a vein in their horses, and drink the blood. They cross every ravine and swim their horses over the rivers.
—anonymous 13th-century description of the Mongols

In his struggle with Arigböge for control of the Mongol Empire, Kublai could count on China's rich agricultural stores, shown here in the terraced rice paddies along the river valleys, to feed his armies.

blai rose from his white horse-skin throne and embraced his brother, wiping the tears off Arigböge's face. He asked his brother to say which one of them had been in the right. Though he regretted the strife between them, Arigböge was unrepentant. Kublai was not offended, however, and admired his brother's courage.

Arigböge's generals were questioned next. Kublai noted that they had caused much confusion and tumult among the Mongol people and asked them to name their own punishment. Arigböge rose to defend his generals, bravely taking all responsibility for the rebellion. But one of Arigböge's generals now rose and addressed his fellow prisoners, saying that they had sworn their lives to put Arigböge on the throne and, having failed, their lives were forfeit.

"Today is a day of dying," he said. "Let us keep our word." Kublai pronounced sentence on those who had rebelled against him. Arigböge's 10 generals were given their wish and were condemned to die.

Sorghaghtani Beki had counseled her sons to stand united. Heeding her words, Kublai now spared his younger brother but ordered that Arigböge not be allowed to see him for a year. He would convene a new khuriltai to decide Arigböge's punishment and at the same time reconfirm his own right to the throne.

Kublai dispatched envoys with a message to the Mongol nobles to come to him. But there was still bitterness and suspicion among them, and those who Kublai summoned were delayed or sought excuses. In 1266, Arigböge died suddenly. The cause of his death is a mystery, though some historians claim the Little One was poisoned.

It was time for Kublai to move against the Sung army and resume his conquest of south China. He was not yet master of the region south of the Yangtze

Besieged on the northern steppes of Mongolia, the armies of Arigböge could not live off the land and had to transport food and supplies long distances through a sparsely settled land and a hostile climate. As a result, many starved.

River. The area was a rich one, with fertile fields and a thriving seaborne trade. In 1267, Kublai ordered his troops to prepare horses and weapons for action. He sent a message to the Sung emperor, as was the custom of the time, formally announcing his intention to wage war.

The previous Sung emperor had reigned for 40 years until, in November 1264, at the age of 62, he died. Because the emperor had no son, his nephew was placed on the throne the following year. The new emperor, Tu-tsung, was a highly cultured man but an incompetent ruler. He placed his land in the hands of worthless ministers who hindered the courageous actions of the Sung army's generals. His prime minister, Chia Ssu-tao, was interested only in gaining power for himself.

Chia Ssu-tao concealed news of the invaders' advances from the emperor and discredited and killed

This Persian painting depicts the warriors of Kublai's armies crossing a river on a kind of primitive pontoon bridge. Control of the rivers and the cities near them was essential to the conquest of southern China.

those who tried to inform Tu-tsung of the danger. One of those who had sought to warn the emperor was Liu Ching, a governor in Sichuan Province. Fearing for his life, Liu Ching took service with the Mongols.

Kublai's advance down the Yangtze was hard won. The turning point for the Mongol army was the siege of Hsiang-yang and Fan-ch'eng, twin cities on either side of the Han River, which flows into the Yangtze farther south. The cities were the last strongholds of the Sung guarding the rich and fertile Yangtze River basin. They were the keys to Kublai's total victory in China.

With a lion's strength they have voices more shrill than an eagle.
—GRIGOR OF AKANC
Armenian monk, on the Mongols

The defenders resisted Kublai's army for five years, inflicting heavy casualties. At first, Kublai had counted on starving the Sung defenders from their strongholds. But the superior Sung navy mounted a bold flotilla that brought arms and provisions down the river. After an unsuccessful blockade, Kublai saw the need to change his tactics.

The two cities were connected by bridges of boats; the river itself was barred with strong chains and armed barges. To overcome the defenders, the Mongols would have to breach the moats and thick protective walls of the twin cities. Kublai knew his losses would be heavy.

Kublai opened the prisons of northern China and released some 20,000 condemned prisoners. Destined to die in any case, they readily accepted the Great Khan's offer of horses, arms, and clothing if they would join his army. Kublai promised to make them emirs and men of standing if they exerted themselves. He gave instructions that they be molded into skillful and loyal warriors.

The troops that Kublai now assembled to converge upon Hsiang-yang and Fan-ch'eng were a multinational force. Throughout his reign, Kublai was successful at attracting non-Mongols to his cause and employing them to achieve his aims. Kublai summoned Uighurs from central Asia to lead his troops and Koreans and Jurchens to build ships. Two Sung generals also served the Great Khan. One of these was Liu Ching, who had defected from the Sung to escape Prime Minister Chia's persecution.

Mongols use siege tactics to attack a typical Chinese walled city. The catapult in the lower left corner of the painting was an instrument of war borrowed from other cultures.

Engineers from Persia were also among Kublai's forces. They supplied Kublai with the weapons he needed to break the enemy's resistance: death-dealing catapults that hurled huge stones into the twin cities. Battered by a barrage of rocks that shattered their walls and crushed their soldiers, the Sung forces could not withstand the Mongol assault. Kublai sent an appeal to the besieged defenders, promising that no harm would come to them if they surrendered. Mongol offers of mercy were notoriously unreliable, but the Sung defenders of the twin cities surrendered to Kublai in late March 1273, bringing to an end a siege that had lasted five years.

Kublai next set his sights on the Sung capital at Hangchow and placed his army under the command of his close friend Bayan, a general descended from a long line of military officers. Bayan's strategy was to take full advantage of the new siege machinery the Mongols had adopted from Persia. He would approach a city and demand the submission of his opponents at once. If they refused, he would attack with a devastating assault of catapults and flamethrowers. As Bayan marched southward, city after city submitted. Some Sung generals realized the futility of fighting against the superior Mongol forces. Others, embittered by the treacherous policies of Minister Chia Ssu-tao, went over to the Mongols.

Chia Ssu-tao found himself discredited with the emperor and tried to regain his prestige by personally leading the Sung army. But his supporters continued to desert him. Chia was stripped of his rank and banished to Fukien Province. En route to Fukien, he was killed by the commander of the Sung detachment sent to escort him.

In 1274, the Emperor Tu-tsung died, and his four-year-old son succeeded him to the throne. But the

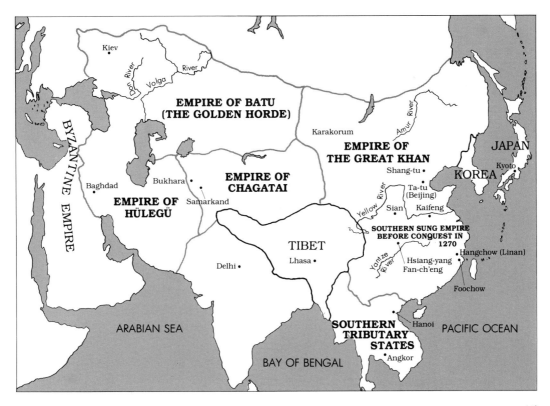

real power of the Sung lay in the hands of the empress dowager, the dead emperor's widow, who was old and in failing health. When Bayan's troops approached Hangchow, she had the emperor's two half brothers escorted from the city and sent south. She and the emperor remained at Hangchow to rally the local defense.

The empress dowager now dispatched envoys to Bayan promising to pay regular tribute if he would withdraw his troops. But Bayan was too close to victory and refused. Finally, the Sung emperor acknowledged himself as Kublai's subject, and the grand seal of the Sung empire was turned over to Bayan. The campaign was over.

"The North and South have become one family," Bayan said as he accepted the Sung submission. The emperor and the empress dowager returned north with him to Kublai's summer capital at Shang-tu. A parade of carts loaded with spoils from the Sung court accompanied them.

Kublai received the young emperor kindly and eventually sent him to be educated in a Buddhist monastery. He was delighted with the prizes of war from the Sung dynasty, but Chabi could not hold back her tears. It had come to her mind that the empire of the Mongols would also finish this way. Kublai asked Chabi to take charge of the empress dowager and her suite. Chabi treated the women generously, gaining much goodwill for Kublai from his newly conquered subjects.

Despite the capture of Hangchow, the conquest of China was still not complete. Sung support now rallied around the captured emperor's two half brothers, who had escaped south when Bayan's troops threatened Hangchow. Sung loyalists crowned the captured emperor's older half brother as Emperor Shih and established a new court at Foochow.

Mongol troops relentlessly pursued the Sung court, and the new emperor was forced to flee. The Sung court boarded a fleet of junks and sailed south. But the court could find no safe resting place. They sailed through the seas of south China for two years. On June 6, 1278, the Sung refugees encoun-

tered a bad storm. The emperor's ship sank, and he barely escaped with his life. The strain was too much for the sickly boy, and he died just before his 10th birthday.

The Sung loyalists rallied one last time. They enthroned the dead emperor's half brother, Ping, as Mongol troops closed in. Early in 1279, Mongol troops caught up with the imperial ship. One of the young emperor's entourage appeared before him. He proclaimed that the empire was doomed, seized the child in his arms, and jumped into the waves.

The Sung dynasty, having ruled China for more than 300 years, had vanished. Kublai Khan was master of the Chinese empire.

This engraving depicts the final tragedy of the Sung dynasty. In 1279, after two years at sea trying to evade Mongol capture, the last Sung ruler, the boy emperor Ping, is thrown to his death at sea by despairing members of the court.

4

The Mongol War Machine

Kublai had completed the conquest of China, the crowning achievement of his career, but there came a new threat from the very heart of his huge empire. The challenge to Kublai's leadership came from his cousin, Khaidu, who ruled central Asia. Khaidu believed that Kublai had betrayed his Mongol heritage and succumbed to the sedentary way of life of the Chinese, who lived mainly in settled, agricultural communities. Khaidu wanted to preserve the traditional nomadic Mongol way of life.

Central Asia functioned as a crossroads for commerce and communications among China, India, the Middle East, and Europe. At the oases of central Asia, trade caravans and messengers stopped to rest and replenish their supplies. This was the famous "Silk Route," stretching from central China all the way to Antioch on the Mediterranean Sea. Control over central Asia was vital to the integrity of Kublai's empire.

They rode over vast tracts of the world, sacking cities and defeating the armies of their enemies, without caring much what the cities were called, or what king they were defeating.
—R. P. LISTER
historian, on the
Mongol armies

Mongol tribesmen move their encampment. Traditional nomadic ways came into conflict with the need to manage China's farmers, and conservative Mongols such as Khaidu challenged Kublai's position on this issue.

Kublai appointed one of his sons by Chabi, Nomukhan, Prince of Pacification of the North. Kublai had slated Nomukhan for a military career, whereas Nomukhan's elder brother, Chen-chin, meaning "true gold," had been chosen to rule as Kublai's heir. Accordingly, Kublai now sent Nomukhan along with several of his princely cousins to central Asia to confront Khaidu.

Khaidu used the traditional Mongol tactic that had worked so successfully for generations. His army harassed Nomukhan's troops but retreated westward to avoid a major confrontation. Nomukhan did fight several skirmishes but made little headway in crushing Khaidu's main force. Kublai sent Chabi's nephew, An-t'ung, to help the beleaguered Nomukhan.

An-t'ung quickly realized the reason for Nomukhan's failure to overcome Khaidu: Factionalism and quarrels divided Nomukhan's forces. Included in Nomukhan's army were two sons of Arigböge and a son of Mangu. Perhaps it was their belief that they had more right to the throne than Kublai, or resentment for what they saw as past wrongs, that motivated these young men. They met secretly, deciding to seize Nomukhan and An-t'ung and turn them over to the enemy. The conspirators carried out their plans, capturing Nomukhan, An-t'ung, and Kököchü, Nomukhan's younger brother.

Khaidu sent a terse message to the conspirators. "We are grateful to you, and it is what we expected of you. Since there is good water and grass in that region, stay where you are." Clearly, though he profited from their actions, Khaidu distrusted men who would betray their own leader and did not want them in his own territory.

Kublai dispatched Bayan to obtain the release of his sons and nephew. Bayan was the general who had met with such success in southern China against the Sung army. But Bayan, too, was unable to engage the enemy in a decisive battle. Eventually, all the hostages were released unharmed, after 10 years in captivity. Kublai then promoted Nomukhan to be Prince of Northern Peace in recognition of his son's travails.

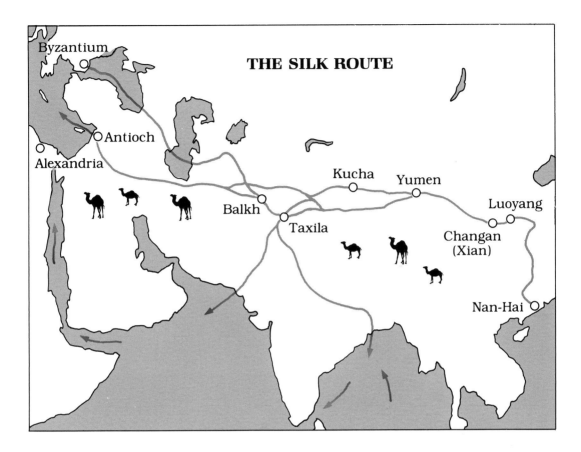

THE SILK ROUTE

Byzantium

Antioch

Alexandria

Balkh

Taxila

Kucha

Yumen

Luoyang

Changan
(Xian)

Nan-Hai

Kublai had to acknowledge that he could not control Khaidu and central Asia. He ordered his troops to retreat to the easily defensible areas of eastern China. Along this border, Kublai stationed troops for defense against Khaidu. He also provided agricultural assistance to the inhabitants of the oasis towns to make them self-sufficient. Kublai thus preserved Mongolia as part of his domain, but central Asia remained in control of Khaidu.

Frightened by possible reprisals from Kublai, the conspirators fled to the Mongolian steppes. Here they launched a series of attacks against Karakorum, the old Mongol capital. But Kublai easily defeated the renegades, who were unable to decide among themselves who should be their supreme ruler.

Kublai's empire had been conquered from the saddle. The success of his army was due to its ability

The famous Silk Route consisted of overland trading routes stretching from eastern China to the Mediterranean Sea, along which caravans brought silk, spices, tea, and ceramics to the West. Khaidu's rebellion in central Asia threatened to disrupt Kublai's control of this commercial activity.

This painting of a Mongolian circus shows riders performing various feats of horsemanship, the skill that made the Mongol conquests possible. Some riders were organized into squadrons of mounted archers; others formed units of light and heavy cavalry armed with lances and swords.

to move swiftly and quickly concentrate its forces. Every battle that Kublai fought was meticulously planned. Because punishments for cowardice were severe, he knew he could count on the discipline and bravery of his troops.

Kublai, however, also believed that even with the best strategic planning and the most disciplined troops, a warrior could not achieve his goal without the help of heaven and his ancestors. Before each campaign, Kublai would perform rituals and make sacrifices to the spirit of his grandfather, Genghis Khan, for victory over his enemies. First he would pour a libation of mare's milk on the ground as an offering. He faced each of the four cardinal directions in turn, crying out Genghis's name to the four corners of the earth. At his signal a magnificent stallion was sacrificed, its throat slashed, staining the ground with blood. The Mongol *beki*, or chief shaman, would work himself into a trance and ride the spirit of the sacrificed horse up to the heavens. He would plead with the Khan's ancestors to grant Kublai victory. Only then did Kublai order the attack.

The harsh conditions of nomadic life gave the Mongol soldiers great endurance. Organization and training turned them from reckless warriors into loyal, disciplined soldiers. They were ready to kill without pity, to follow orders with unquestioning obedience, and to suffer without complaint.

The organization of Kublai's army would not be unfamiliar to a soldier today. It was a highly organized fighting group with a strict chain of command, complete with intelligence gatherers and quartermasters for supplies. Its fighting units were organized in multiples of 10. A unit of 10 men was called an *arban*; 10 arbans formed a *jargun* of 100 men. Ten jarguns formed a regiment of 1,000 men called a *minghan*, and 10 minghans formed a 10,000-man division called a *tumen*. The soldiers marched with silk banners displaying Kublai's sun-and-moon emblem. All men in the Mongol empire over the age of 20 were liable for military service, except for physicians, priests, and those who washed the bodies of the dead.

The backbone of the Mongol army was the individual, keen-eyed archer mounted on a swift Mongol horse. Horses were respected comrades-in-arms.

A modern-day Mongolian rider practices the ancient art of horse catching. Horses and other animals were a measure of a warrior's wealth, and skill in obtaining them was a matter of pride. In many respects, ancient Mongol culture could be compared to that of the Plains Indians of North America.

Their harnesses and saddles were richly decorated with silver ornaments. When a soldier died in battle, his favorite horse was killed and buried with him. The Mongols believed the two spirits could ride together in heaven.

The bow was the Mongol soldier's most important weapon. He carried two bows, a short one for use when mounted and a longer bow for use on foot. The larger bow had a range of more than 200 yards. Made from layers of horn and sinew on a wooden frame and covered with waterproof lacquer, these weapons enabled the mounted warrior to injure his enemy without closing with him, thereby avoiding

the bloody hand-to-hand fighting with swords, axes, and pikes that stalemated the medieval armies of Europe at this same time. The bow and arrow, as much as the horse, meant mobility on the battlefield. A stone ring worn on the thumb enabled the archer to shoot with strength and accuracy, even from horseback.

In his quiver each soldier carried a variety of arrows. Armor-piercing arrows were more than a yard long, with tips of tempered, or hardened, iron. Warriors also carried incendiary arrows, arrows tipped with grenades, long- and short-range arrows, and whistling arrows used for identifying targets and signaling other troops.

Equipment was simple and easily carried in a man's saddlebags. In his kit the soldier carried a file for sharpening the tips of his arrows, a hatchet, a coil of rope, fishhooks and line, and other tools to repair his equipment. He also carried a change of clothing and a waterproof leather bag that he used as a life jacket for crossing rivers.

Astride his horse and riding at a full gallop, the Mongol archer could shoot in any direction with deadly force and accuracy. His stirrups supported him as he strung his arrows and fired. He timed his release to come between the jarring footfalls of his horse.

On the march, each soldier had at least 3 mounts and sometimes as many as 20. He could change horses and ride for days at a time, eating in the saddle. Traveling this way, Mongol cavalry could cover 200 miles in about 3 days.

The men wore blue or brown tunics called *kalats*, with trousers of blue or gray. In the winter they were lined with fur. Their flat leather boots had no heels and laced up the front. Light cavalry wore a quilted kalat or a cuirass, an armored breastplate made of lacquered leather strips. Heavy cavalry wore coats of chain mail, with a cuirass of hide or iron scales covered in leather.

Every soldier was required to wear a long silk undershirt next to his skin. If an enemy arrow pierced his armor, the tough silk material would enfold itself around the arrow as it penetrated. By carefully pull-

> *The Mongol conquerors faced the age-old problem of how to rule in a Chinese fashion and still retain power.*
> —JOHN FAIRBANK
> historian

ing on the silk, the arrowhead could be extracted, painfully, but without making the wound any worse. Many of their enemies, seeing the Mongol warriors pull arrows from their bodies in this way, thought that they were superhuman and invincible. All the same, wounds were often filthy, and it was common for soldiers to die of infection. Mongols, raised on the dry steppes, rarely washed. When they did wash themselves, it was with the urine of their horses. They often wore their silk shirts until they began to rot from accumulated sweat and grime.

The armor and weapons used by Mongolian heavy cavalry and infantry. As he moved south in his conquest of China, Kublai enlisted many non-Mongols into his armies, and harassing cavalry tactics gave way to the shock force of massive, heavily armored infantry assaults and long sieges.

Communicating orders was a serious concern in commanding an army of thousands of warriors, the majority of whose officers did not read or write. The Mongol army developed a variety of signaling devices, easily discernible from long distances in the heat of battle. Simple messages were relayed from unit to unit by a system of waving flags, a precursor of the semaphore system used well into the 20th century. The officers repeated the signal with their swords. At night, lanterns and flaming arrows were used.

The Mongolian helmet was simple in design, but the fine metalwork here and on suits of armor reveals a high level of craftsmanship. The Mongols, who could be absolutely merciless in victory, always spared those individuals who exhibited practical skills.

Attributed to Ch'iu Ying, a Ming dynasty artist who painted more than 150 years after the collapse of the Mongol Empire, this naturalistic scroll painting shows Mongol horsemen on a hunt.

The Mongol's favorite battle tactic was the *manoudai*. Light cavalry would charge the enemy alone, break ranks, and then flee. The enemy would usually give chase, convinced that the advantage was theirs. By the time they realized their mistake, they would be spread out thinly, easy targets for the deadly accurate Mongol archers. When the quivers of the Mongol archers were empty, the signal was given to the Mongol heavy cavalry.

The charge of the heavy cavalry was the final deadly blow that usually crushed the Mongol's enemies. The horsemen advanced in total silence, their mounts trotting in strict formation. At the last possible moment, the fateful signal was sounded on the *naccara*, a large kettle drum carried to the battlefield on the back of a camel. With a hideous war cry, the Mongol troops galloped to the slaughter. Like animals on the Great Hunt, not a man could escape the circle of death-dealing warriors. The devastation was total, and the Mongol attackers were without mercy.

Where terrain made it difficult to deploy the fearsome Mongol cavalry, archers shot containers filled with burning tar or arrows with explosives attached. One common ploy was to put felt puppets dressed in armor on spare horses. The enemy would be duped into believing that the Mongols had a much larger force. Troops concealed their movements by setting dry grass on fire or raising clouds of dust.

The Mongol army also developed tactics for attacking towns and cities surrounded by walls, a type of fortification that Kublai had encountered at Hangchow. Archers shot incendiary arrows filled with naphtha and quicklime over the walls, creating pandemonium among the defenders. The Mongols also used rockets made from bamboo wrapped in leather. Though the explosion of these rockets was terrifying, the damage was more psychological than physical, since they were unreliable and woefully inaccurate.

The Mongol army also employed engineers to build dams, cutting off the enemy's essential water supplies. Other engineers dug tunnels and placed mines under fortified walls or built siege engines capable of launching huge missiles such as those that had been used to conquer the twin cities of Hsiang-yang and Fan-ch'eng. Such machines required crews of 40 men to create tension on their launching ropes.

The Mongols also engaged in psychological warfare and intelligence gathering. Spies collected information from which generals were able to draw up maps and study the best routes for campaigns. Other spies disguised as merchants were sent into enemy territory to terrorize the defenders with tales of Mongol strength and ferocity. Still others were sent to persuade the people of the area that the Mongols would be more sympathetic rulers than their own local governors and that they should therefore surrender without a fight.

Kublai had used this deadly, disciplined fighting force to forge his empire as city after city submitted to his ruthless armies. But what came after conquest? Now the question was whether Kublai could rule in peace the lands he had subjugated by force.

5

The Middle Kingdom

When Kublai proclaimed himself emperor of China, he turned to the Chinese classic the I Ching, or *Book of Changes* in his search for an auspicious name for his new dynasty. He called the dynasty Yüan, meaning the origin of the universe.

In fact, it was China that had conquered Kublai. She simply absorbed the Mongols into her huge population and bent them to her traditional ways. China's ancient, sophisticated culture did what her army could not do and subdued the Mongol hordes. The Chinese called their country the Middle Kingdom. For the Chinese, this meant that their nation was at the center of world civilization. Kublai came to share their worldview.

Chinese emperors believed that they ruled by the Mandate of Heaven. They performed rites every spring to ask for the blessings of heaven to ensure a good harvest, peace, and prosperity throughout the empire. The Mandate of Heaven was bestowed on the emperor for his righteous rule. If the emperor acted unrighteously, the mandate could be withdrawn by heaven or his own subjects, who had the right to depose an unjust ruler. Often, natural disasters or cataclysmic human events were perceived

The ruling house of the Yuan dynasty was a foreign one, Mongol, and this has always been a deterrent to proper and full Chinese appreciation.
—SHERMAN LEE historian, on Chinese resistance to Mongol culture during Kublai's reign

A Chinese engraving depicts Kublai Khan as a wise and benevolent Confucian ruler. Measured either in terms of lands or people conquered, his was the largest empire in history ever to be ruled by one man.

by the Chinese as warnings of heaven's displeasure with unrighteous or incompetent rule. The emperor could then perform rituals of purification and issue a statement of self-criticism in the hope of maintaining the mandate and the faith of his people. The emperor was also supposed to implement policies to improve the situation that had provoked heaven's wrath.

Kublai had declared himself the legitimate successor of the fallen Sung emperors. Now his task was to prove to his new subjects that he indeed enjoyed the Mandate of Heaven. Using the administrative talents learned from his mother, Sorghaghtani Beki, and the military talents of his grandfather, Genghis Khan, Kublai became an excellent statesman as well as a warrior, coupling the Mongol name not only with dread but also with constructive government.

The court of T'ai-tsung, the second emperor of the Tang dynasty, who was renowned for his wise and compassionate reign. Chabi urged Kublai to model himself after such a ruler to gain favor with his Chinese subjects.

Kublai's wife Chabi encouraged him to learn about the Chinese emperor T'ai-tsung of the Tang dynasty, who had ruled a powerful and prosperous China during the 7th century. Chabi invited Confucian scholars to come to Kublai's court to explain T'ai-tsung's superb accomplishments to the new emperor. Kublai realized that if he wished to govern China well, he had to identify himself with and emulate a respected figure in Chinese tradition.

Kublai faced enormous problems. China had still not recovered from the devastation caused by the wars to control her. Much arable land lay fallow, and people were now starving. War had reduced the Chinese population from 100 million to less than 60 million. The Chinese peasants were uncertain about the intentions of their new ruler and afraid that Kublai would expropriate their lands for pasture. However, Kublai redistributed the land, allotting the farmers larger plots. He gave them seeds and tools to increase their productivity. As conditions improved, Kublai established reserves of grain in all the major towns to safeguard against future famine. Kublai knew that the stability of his empire rested on a productive and prosperous agricultural class. He set up schools to teach farming methods and encouraged literacy among the farming com-

Among his many enlightened policies, Kublai sought to protect his subjects from bad harvests by establishing large grain reserves like those on this modern-day Chinese commune. Droughts and floods were a common experience for Chinese peasants, and millions died from resulting famine.

A section of the Grand Canal, built by Kublai to transport goods from the rich regions of the south to his northern capital at Ta-tu. The Mongol court stayed in northern China, partly because of the south's uncomfortably hot climate and partly so that ties with the Mongol way of life would not be broken.

munity. He also introduced public assistance and opened homes for the needy and the old.

Beijing in northern China was rebuilt as Ta-tu, Kublai's splendid capital. The vast palace of Kublai lay in the heart of the city, whose wide, straight avenues were laid out on a square grid. Hangchow in southern China, the capital of the Sung dynasty that Kublai had ordered his troops not to destroy, became the cultural capital of China; Ta-tu served as the administrative center of his empire.

To link the 2 cities together, Kublai ordered that the Yangtze River be extended 135 miles to the north by constructing the Grand Canal. Boat transportation from south to north via the Grand Canal was much safer and more economical than sea transportation, where there was always the danger of typhoons.

Vast quantities of supplies would have to be shipped north via the Grand Canal, for there was not enough farmland around Ta-tu to supply food to the swelling population of the new capital. Three million laborers took part in the construction of the Grand Canal. Kublai spent vast sums of money to link the granaries of the Yangtze River region to his capital. Even today, long stretches of the Grand Canal are still used to transport goods in China. The Grand Canal remains a great feat of engineering and construction, second only to the Great Wall.

Kublai wanted his capital at Ta-tu to symbolize his desire to become an emperor of China and not just her conqueror. The city was modeled on the plan for an ideal capital found in an ancient Chinese text. Still, Kublai never forgot that the roots of the Mongols were planted firmly in the steppes. He ordered steppe grass to be planted in an area within his palace at Ta-tu. He also sent for soil and grass from the Mongol homeland with which to cover his ancestral altar in the palace. Kublai participated in Mongol rituals and employed Mongol shamans to pray for prosperity. Kublai's sons and their cousins lived in yurts erected in the imperial parks rather than in the palace itself. When one of Kublai's wives was pregnant, she moved into one of the yurts to give birth.

As a nomad of the steppes, Kublai had moved his home each season to find good pasture and shelter for his flocks. As emperor of China, he continued

Kublai pitched his yurts inside his fabled city of Ta-tu much as this modern-day Mongolian pitched his traditional yurt inside a paved courtyard.

his seasonal migration on a magnificent scale. He built a summer retreat at Shang-tu, and the entire court traveled to this marble summer palace each year to enjoy the cool breezes of the Khingan Mountains that swept through its rooms. At Shang-tu, 10,000 white mares provided milk to make Kublai's koumiss. Kublai called this drink "the wine of heaven." Parks with rare animals and splendid pavilions were constructed for Kublai's enjoyment.

Each autumn, the imperial court made its way from Shang-tu back to Ta-tu. Kublai traveled in a two-wheeled carriage made of gold and studded with precious jewels. The interior of the carriage was lined with the skins of rare animals, and the carriage itself was drawn by four richly ornamented elephants and four white horses.

Kublai raised revenue for his luxuries and great public works by continuing the traditional Chinese practice of government monopolies on salt, iron, silver, gold, and jade. He sought to impose monopolies on tea and liquor, but these steps proved too

This drawing shows the various stages of mining and processing salt. Kublai monopolized control of salt production in China, and the salt tax proved to be one of his most valuable sources of revenue. Marco Polo may even have served for a time as one of his tax collectors.

A jade carving of a dragon from the period of Kublai's reign, known as the Yüan dynasty, revealing both the wealth to be had by the conquerors and their reverence for skilled craftsmanship. Kublai did much to encourage the arts.

difficult to implement, particularly in southern China, and were abandoned.

In theory, the Confucian system practiced by the preceding Chinese dynasties had been a meritocracy, a system of government by the most talented. Government posts were awarded on the basis of open and competitive imperial examinations held each year. By doing well on the examinations, an individual — regardless of family background or class origins — could rise to the top of the civil service. Memorization of Confucian doctrines was the key to passing these exams. But in truth the subjects that a future minister had to study and excel at — the arts, classical Chinese literature and poetry, moral philosophy, calligraphy — had little to do with the proper management of government. Kublai, having seen for himself the true corruption and incompetence of the old dynasty he had conquered, abolished the Confucian examination system. This gave the new emperor a freer hand in choosing competent and pragmatic advisers whose views would not be shaped by one ideology or by the intrigues of the court.

Kublai did have many Confucian advisers, however, and often adopted their recommendations. His chief Chinese adviser was named Liu Ping-chung. It was Liu who had suggested the name Yüan for Kublai's new dynasty. Also at Liu's suggestion, Kublai had moved his capital from Karakorum to Tatu in order to be closer to the heartland of his empire. Kublai also had his designated heir, Chenchin, tutored in the Confucian classics. But a return

Now the Capital Museum of Beijing, this building was originally a Confucian temple built during Kublai's reign. Kublai walked a fine line with the Confucians, wanting to establish himself as a truly Chinese ruler but fearing their loyalty to the deposed Sung emperors.

to the traditional system of Chinese government was not Kublai's aim.

Kublai wanted a government that would preserve Mongol dominance and not grant too much power to the Chinese, particularly the newly conquered southern Chinese, who might still harbor Sung loyalties. In place of the elaborate imperial bureaucracy, Kublai substituted a system based on personal loyalty and responsibility. His basic policy was to establish a straightforward system of rewards and punishments. He actively solicited suggestions from his officials, allowing those who presented memorials to seal the envelopes. A memorial was a petition to the emperor to take note of some problem. By sealing the envelope, a petitioner was assured that his complaint would reach the ears of the emperor himself and not some underling who might have reason to hide the truth from the Son of Heaven, as had often been the case with the Sung emperors. Furthermore, if the proposals in the memorial were not adopted, there would be no punishment. If the proposals were useful, Kublai would liberally reward the person who made them, hoping to encourage honesty, loyalty, and sincerity.

Kublai knew that his new policies would generate some resentment, particularly with the Confucians among the southern Chinese. In order to gain their favor, Kublai ordered the Great Temple to be built near his palace in Ta-tu. The building of the temple signaled that Kublai intended to continue the rituals associated with ancestor worship that were basic to Confucian philosophy. At the same time, to avoid alienating some conservative Mongols and to show that he had not abandoned his heritage, Kublai also built altars for the annual sacrifices that were part of the Mongol rituals at each year's end.

Kublai pursued a policy designed to win over all the major religions in his realm. Tolerance of all creeds had been the lesson that his mother, Sorghaghtani Beki, had encouraged him to learn in the first appanage he ruled. Muslims, Buddhists, Taoists, and Christians were all welcome at his court. Kublai was anxious to find favor with the Muslims, who promoted trade with the rest of Asia and brought considerable wealth to the imperial treasury. Taoism's reputed magical powers and the Taoists' experiments in alchemy and astrology also fascinated Kublai. He knew that Taoism had great appeal to many of his subjects, so he supplied funds for the construction of Taoist temples, and the Taoists in turn proved to be very loyal. They had not forgotten that Kublai's grandfather, Genghis, had practiced Taoism. They aided Kublai in performing yearly rituals at Mount Tai, one of the duties expected of a Chinese emperor.

Earlier, Kublai had favored Buddhism because of his wife Chabi's ardent Buddhist beliefs. Of all the branches of Buddhism, Tibetan Buddhism seemed to have tremendous appeal for Kublai. Kublai invited the 'Phags-pa lama of the Sa-skya sect of Tibetan Buddhism to his court and gave him an official appointment. Many in the Buddhist community began to perceive Kublai not only as the emperor of China but also as a religiously inspired model for the universal ruler. The 'Phags-pa lama suggested the initiation of annual Buddhist rituals at the court to destroy demons and protect the empire. Kublai performed these rituals side by side with Mongolian, Confucian, and Taoist rites in pursuit of his policy to win over all the religions in his realm.

Kublai's efforts to be perceived as the legitimate emperor of China enjoyed much success. His good works and the support of various religious groups put him in good favor with much of the population. The strongest resistance to his legitimacy came, understandably, from southern China, which was the last region added to his empire. The Confucians of southern China could never forgive Kublai for robbing them of their special position at court, a privilege they had enjoyed under the Sung for more than three centuries.

Throughout his reign, Kublai tried to maintain a delicate balance between promoting the interests of his Chinese subjects and exploiting China's resources for his own glory and renown. It was a problem no different from that faced by any Chinese emperor, but he had made a good start.

He struggled to maintain a balance between the highly developed culture of China and the less sophisticated expressions of his own people.
—MORRIS ROSSABI
American historian, on
Kublai during the
Yuan dynasty

Ye Book of Ser Marco Polo ye Venetian

concerning ye kingdoms of ye East:

Newly done into English
by HENRY YULE c.b.

Second VOL.

Edition 1ST.

Messer Marco Polo with Messer Nicolo and Messer Maffeo returned from XXVI years sojourn in the Orient, is denied entrance to the Ca Polo see Introd

LONDON: JOHN MURRAY:
1874

6

Marco Polo and the Great Khan

In the middle of the 13th century, trade along the Silk Route began to flourish again. This fragile line of overland trading routes, stretching from China through the oases of central Asia, the towns and marketplaces of Persia, and finally to the ports of the eastern Mediterranean, had been closed to European merchants for hundreds of years by hostile Muslim governments. To the people of the West, China was a great mystery and Japan completely unknown. But with the conquests of Genghis and Kublai, the Silk Route was now protected by the Mongol army. Precious goods wound their way in caravans of camels across remote deserts and mountains, from oasis town to oasis town. Camels, the ships of the desert, could easily adapt to the rough terrain the Silk Route followed. They could endure extreme heat and carry heavy loads. At watering holes they drank their fill, then continued for days without drinking. Their flat hooves kept them from sinking into the sand.

The greatest lord that ever was born in the world or that now is.
—MARCO POLO
Venetian traveler, on
Kublai Khan

One of the earliest English editions of *The Book of Marco Polo*, the incredible story of his travels through Kublai Khan's empire. The cover illustration shows the returning Polos unable to gain entrance to their own house in Venice. They had been away for 20 years and were not recognized.

71

In Italy, the seagoing trading cities of Venice and Genoa began to establish stations on the Black Sea and on the eastern Mediterranean. Enticed by tales of fabulous riches, merchants from these cities cast their nets wider and wider for the goods of Asia. Silk, spices, tea, and pottery were in strong demand in Europe.

In Venice there lived two merchant brothers named Niccoló and Maffeo Polo. When trading in the central Asian city of Bukhara, they chanced to meet with officials of Kublai's government. These officials had been sent by the Great Khan to encourage trade relations with the West and to open official relations with the Vatican. Seizing the opportunity, the Polo brothers set off for China with the officials and in 1260 stood before Kublai at his court at Ta-tu. Kublai, who had never seen Europeans before, was delighted to meet them and requested that they ask the pope to send 100 scholars to Kublai's court. The Great Khan wished to be fully informed about Europe.

When the two brothers returned to Italy in 1269, the situation in Rome had changed. Pope Clement IV had died the previous year and no new pope had been elected. The College of Cardinals could not settle on a successor. After waiting for two years, their frustration mounted. The Polos desired to return to Kublai Khan's court as quickly as possible. The Polos called China *Cathay*, a word derived from the Turkish *Khitai* or *Kitat*, the name of the people who had ruled over northern China during the 11th century.

Finally, in 1271, the Polo brothers set off again for the lands of the Great Khan. They had obtained neither the papal blessing nor the 100 scholars Kublai had requested. They did, however, bring something that Kublai was to treasure highly. The Polos brought with them Niccoló's son, Marco. Marco, who was 17 years old, was eager for adventure. He was enthralled by tales of the faraway Asian lands, listened carefully as his father and uncle described their first meeting with Kublai Khan, and yearned to see the Great Khan's court for himself. The three Polos reached Kublai's court in 1275.

He is a man of good stature, neither short nor tall but of moderate height. His limbs are well fleshed out and modelled in due proportion. His complexion is fair and ruddy like a rose, the eyes black and handsome, the nose shapely and set squarely in place.

—MARCO POLO
Venetian traveler, on meeting Kublai

An engraving of Marco Polo as a mature, worldly, wise middle-aged man. He must have appeared that way to Europeans after his journey, though he was only a boy of 17 when his uncle and father took him to China.

All traders of that time had to conduct their business in many languages, and the Polos were no exception. Marco, who was more of a young scholar than a merchant and who was determined to make a good impression on Kublai, at once set about mastering the Mongol tongue. He practiced each day, enlarging his vocabulary and polishing his accent. When the Polos reached Kublai's summer residence at Shang-tu and Marco was presented to the Great Khan, he had already prepared a speech of greeting in Kublai's own tongue.

The meeting was a success, especially for the young Marco. A court official later wrote: "They knelt before him and made obeisance with the utmost humility. The Great Khan bade them rise and received them honorably and entertained them with good cheer. He asked many questions about their condition and how they had fared after their departure. . . . When the Great Khan saw Marco, he asked who he was. 'Sire,' said Messer Niccoló, 'he is my son, and your liege man.' 'He is heartily welcome,' said the Khan."

Marco for his part was favorably impressed by the Khan and described him as "a man of good stature, neither short nor tall but of moderate height. His

The overland route that the Polos took to China paralleled the Silk Route. Given the hazards of 13th-century travel, it is not surprising that their journey took several years.

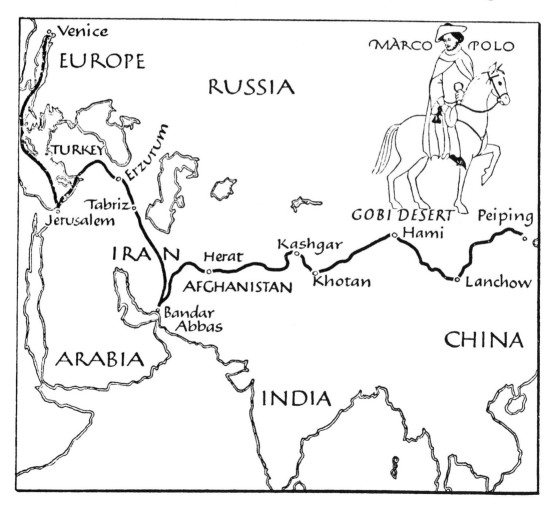

limbs are well fleshed out and modelled in due proportion. His complexion is fair and ruddy like a rose,
the eyes black and handsome, the nose shapely and
set squarely in place."

The Polos were housed in the palace at Ta-tu.
Marco would call the city Khan-balik, meaning the
city of the Great Khan. He immediately set about
learning more of the different languages spoken
throughout the lands that Kublai ruled. From the
8th century onward, Arabs, Turks, and Persians
had settled in large numbers in the northwest and
in the ports of southeast China, serving as inter-
mediaries in the commerce by land and by sea
across Eurasia.

Marco shared with Kublai a passion for falconry,
the training of falcons to hunt, a sport that was
popular among the aristocracy of Europe, the Middle East, and Asia. Kublai invited Marco to accompany him on a hunting expedition. Hunting for the
Mongols was a way to train soldiers and reveal men's
character, and the Great Khan carefully observed
Marco's conduct during the hunt to test his abilities
and learn his temperament. On a typical hunt, as
Marco described it, the Khan "stood on top of a
wooden tower, full of crossbowmen and archers,
which was carried by four elephants wearing stout
leather armor draped with cloths of silk and gold.
Above his head flew his banner with the emblem of
the sun and moon, so high that it could be clearly
seen on every side." So impressed was Kublai with
this young man that he immediately took Marco into
his service.

Marco would serve Kublai as a friend and close
adviser for 17 years. The Khan had faith in Marco's
honesty and his keen powers of observation and
would frequently send him on inspection tours of
the empire. Unlike many earlier rulers of China,
Kublai was always anxious to hear about the life of
his subjects and the conditions under which they
lived. For Marco too, it was the perfect opportunity
to explore and learn about this vast country.

Marco was fascinated by the things he saw in
China that were unknown in Europe. Among the
many wonders he described were coal, "a sort of

Mongol nobles practice the sport of falconry. Falconry was also popular with Europeans, Marco Polo included, and their mutual love of the sport brought Kublai and Marco closer together.

black stone, which is dug out of veins in hillsides and burns like logs," and asbestos, which Marco called "salamander." From China, the Europeans of this time would also discover gunpowder, and from Chinese noodles the Italians would learn to make pasta.

In his travels Marco began to put together a complete economic and geographic sketch of Kublai's realm, describing the trade and wealth of the Great Khan's empire as well as a number of curiosities at Kublai's court. Later, he would write for European readers that "the revenue accruing to the Great Khan . . . is so stupendous that, unless it were seen, it could scarcely be credited." And sure enough, many did not believe, nicknaming the explorer Marco "Millions" for his extravagant tales of the wealth of China.

Kublai recognized the importance of commerce and offered merchants a higher social status than they had enjoyed under the Sung dynasty. During the years of the Mongol conquests, merchant associations had raised money for loans to Mongol nobility. Now Kublai rewarded them. To facilitate trade, he revived the Sung use of paper money, forcing all gold and silver to be turned over to the court. "It is in this city of Khan-balik that the Great Khan has his mint," wrote Marco, "and it is so organized that you might well say that he has mastered the art of alchemy." Marco compared the bustling markets of Chinese cities with those of the great ports of the Western world, such as Venice, his home. Coming from Venice, Marco was particularly impressed with the Chinese system of transporting goods by water and with the Grand Canal that Kublai had built in order to ship grain to his capital at Ta-tu from southern China.

Marco also described the system of paved roads the Khan had built to connect the far reaches of his empire. "Along the main highways frequented by his messengers and by merchants and other folk, he has ordered trees to be planted on both sides, two paces distant from one another. They are so large that they can be seen from a long way off. And he has done this so that any wayfarer may recognize the roads and not lose his way . . . they are a great boon to travellers and traders."

What captured the imagination of Europeans, however, were the tales of Kublai Khan's splendid palaces and lavish ceremonies. Marco described Kublai's palace at Ta-tu as a wondrous place. "Inside, the walls of the halls and chambers are all covered with gold and silver and decorated with pictures of dragons and birds and horsemen and various breeds of beasts and scenes of battle. The ceiling is similarly adorned, so that there is nothing to be seen anywhere but gold and pictures. The hall is so vast and so wide that a meal might well be served there for more than 6,000 men. . . . The roof is all ablaze with scarlet and green and blue and yellow and all the colors that are, so brilliantly varnished that it glitters like crystal and the sparkle of it can be seen from far away."

On his birthday, he dons a magnificent robe of beaten gold. And fully 12,000 barons and knights robe themselves with him in a similar colour and style.
—MARCO POLO
Venetian traveler, on
Kublai Khan

Even today, Marco's description of Kublai's New Year's celebrations stretch the imagination. "On this day the Great Khan receives gifts of more than 100,000 white horses of great beauty and price. And on this day also there is a procession of his elephants, fully 5,000 in number, all draped in fine cloths embroidered with beasts and birds. Each one bears on its back two strong-boxes of great beauty and price filled with the Khan's plate and with costly apparel for his white-robed court. With them come innumerable camels also draped with cloths and laden with provisions for the feast. They all parade

Camel caravans loaded with trade goods still ply the deserts of central Asia. In Kublai's time, this was the West's only source of products from and information about China.

in front of the Great Khan, and it is the most splendid sight that ever was seen. On the morning of this feast, before the tables are set up, all the kings and all the dukes, marquises and counts, barons, knights, astrologers, physicians, falconers, and many other officials and rulers of men and lands and armies appear before the Khan in the great hall. . . . And when they are all seated, each in his proper station, up stands a great dignitary and proclaims in a loud voice: 'Bow down and worship!' No sooner has he said this than they bow down, then and there, and touch the ground with their foreheads, and address a prayer to the lord and worship him as if he were a god."

Marco served at the court of the Great Khan for 17 years. But the Great Khan was growing old. Kublai had enforced a regime tolerant of all people and religions, but nobody knew how foreigners would be treated by the next ruler. Besides, Marco was now in his thirties. He had worked in Kublai's service for almost half his life. It was time to go home.

When Marco made his wishes known, Kublai was reluctant at first to let his trusted friend leave. Finally, after several more requests, Kublai granted Marco permission to return to Venice after one more mission in his service. Marco was to accompany a newly married Mongol princess to the home of her new husband in Persia. Having discharged this last duty faithfully, Marco and his father Niccoló and his uncle Maffeo, after an extraordinary journey, arrived back in Italy in 1295.

When the Polos returned home, neither friends nor family recognized the three men, who were clothed in shabby garments after their long and arduous journey. Finally, the family was convinced that the three ragged travelers were indeed their returned relatives. They gave orders for a splendid feast to be prepared. At the end of the banquet, the story goes, the three men, still clothed in their tattered garments, ripped open the seams of their coats to let fall a shower of emeralds, diamonds, and rubies that Kublai had presented to them upon their departure from China.

After three years in Venice, Marco volunteered to serve as a "gentleman commander" aboard a Venetian galley in the war against Venice's old trading rival, the city of Genoa. He was captured in a naval battle and sent to a Genoese prison. Here, to pass the time, he told his fellow prisoners about his adventures in the service of Kublai Khan. Among the prisoners was Rusticello of Pisa, a romance writer of considerable fame. Marco dictated his story to Rusticello, and with the Pisan's help, Marco Polo's *Book of Wonders* took form.

In his book, Marco revealed a world almost wholly unknown to Western Christendom. More than eighty 14th- and 15th-century manuscripts of Marco's *Book of Wonders* are known. There are 41 Latin editions, 21 in Italian, 16 in French, 6 in German, and even 1 in Irish. There was apparently no English translation until as late as 1579. The book fired the imagination of Europe's bankers, traders, geographers, and explorers. Christopher Columbus had a well-worn copy in his library at Genoa, marked with copious notes.

Modern scholarship has questioned some of Marco's extravagant claims. It would not have been possible for him to have assisted at the siege of Hsiang-

When his gout began to act up or when he wanted to impress visitors, Kublai would travel in a wooden tower mounted on four elephants.

This miniature painting depicts the Polos taking their leave after more than two decades of service to the Great Khan. Kublai was reluctant to let Marco go but finally relented. The journey home was mostly by sea.

yang and Fan-ch'eng, since the twin cities fell in 1273, years before Marco set out from Venice for Kublai's court. Nor is it likely that Marco served as governor of Yangchow. More likely, he may have held a minor post in the salt-tax bureau of that city. Rusticello, the romance writer, may have embellished Marco's story. In any case, even the true stories were so fabulous that Europeans had trouble believing.

What is certain is that the trust, goodwill, and protection that Kublai extended to Marco allowed him to provide Western readers with their first de-

scription of the fabulous splendors of the East, and especially of Kublai's two magnificent courts, the imperial palace at Ta-tu and the summer capital at Shang-tu that Coleridge immortalized in his poem "Xanadu."

Marco had served Kublai Khan at the height of Mongol power, when the Mongol empire was at its zenith. This remarkable friendship with the son of a merchant from a faraway land is evidence of the Great Khan's tolerance and intellectual curiosity and his power to capture the loyalty of the many different people who served him.

7

From Conqueror to Patron

A nation may be conquered by the sword, but building a dynasty requires a degree of wisdom. Kublai had worked to increase the economic prosperity of China's farmers and merchants, but he also had to show that the Mongols could appreciate and preserve China's ancient culture. He knew that he needed to wipe out forever his image as a barbarian from the north if he was ever to be accepted as a Son of Heaven and the legitimate ruler of China. He set about becoming a great patron of the arts and sciences, hoping to link his name with the long and rich tradition of Chinese culture.

The Mongols had been constantly on the move during their conquests and never developed an indigenous group of craftsmen. They did, however, value artisans highly. During their wars of conquest, when a defeated town was put to the sword, all the inhabitants were killed except for the skilled craftsmen. Victorious, the Mongols now craved luxuries and needed craftsmen and skilled workers to reconstruct the cities they had devastated.

Kublai refrained from styling himself the Conqueror of China, and, succumbing to the ancient civilization of his new realm, captured by its symbols and customs which dated from immemorial antiquity, gradually abandoned the national traditions of his own race to accept the age-long traditions of the Middle Kingdom.
—MICHAEL PRAWDIN
historian

This naturalistic painting on silk paper shows Kublai and Chabi on a hunt. The white horse-skin robe identifies the Great Khan. Above, a trader leads his camels through the barren steppes of Mongolia.

The construction of Kublai's capitals at Ta-tu and Shang-tu required vast armies of artisans, whom Kublai favored with rations of food, clothing, and salt. He made various artisans a hereditary class, thereby ensuring that their wealth and skills would be passed on to the next generation. He established a Bureau for Imperial Manufactures charged with providing jewelry, clothing, and textiles for use at his court.

The best-known craftsman in Kublai's court was a Nepali named Aniko, whom the 'Phags-pa lama had brought to the emperor's attention. He was first ordered to repair a human figure made of copper that was used in teaching acupuncture. Kublai was so impressed with Aniko's restoration that he assigned him to work on a number of construction projects — an ancestral shrine, a Buddhist temple, and a pavilion in the park at Ta-tu. Aniko also made exquisite gold and jade jewelry for Chabi. So delighted was Chabi with his work that she arranged his marriage to a well-born Chinese lady and granted him some land.

This portrait of Kublai's wife Chabi, painted during her lifetime, shows the rich ornamentation of the headdresses preferred by Mongolian noblewomen.

Chinese ceramics, plates, and pottery were highly valued and in great demand. Kublai immediately saw the potential for deriving revenue from the export of what even today we call "china," and he began to organize and regulate ceramics production. Trade was particularly heavy with Southeast Asia and the Middle East, although some pottery did eventually reach Europe. The kiln sites, near the fine harbors on China's southeast coast, aided foreign export considerably.

Under the Sung dynasty, ceramics production had been outstanding, but the insistence of the Sung court on adherence to classical forms had stifled creativity. Kublai's potters were not confined by this aesthetic and could experiment freely with shapes, colors, and glazes. One result of these experiments was the appearance of the beautiful blue-and-white porcelain that was to achieve such fame in the subsequent Ming dynasty.

Kublai had the entire Sung imperial painting collection transported to Ta-tu, where it provided the foundation for his own collection. He did not wait for artists to offer him their services but sent emissaries to seek them out and bring them to his court. He commissioned an official portrait of himself that is now in the National Palace Museum in Taipei, Taiwan. Another painting, also now in Taiwan, shows Kublai and his wife Chabi on horseback, enjoying the hunt. The horse, the foundation of Mongol nomadic culture, figures prominently in Mongol art.

Though Kublai did support many Chinese painters, just as many turned down his offers of patronage. Chinese landscape painters in particular were drawn from the circle of Confucian scholars who were still loyal Sung subjects at heart, and many refused to collaborate with Kublai's court. Such painters became *i-min*, or "leftover" subjects, rejecting completely the rule of the Mongol emperor. Large numbers of i-min resided in regions of southern China and now used their painting to express their sorrow at the destruction of the Sung and to extol the virtues of the lost dynasty. One artist, Cheng Ssu-hsiao, was known for his paintings of the Chinese orchid, which he always depicted with-

To rule the sedentary civilizations [Kublai] had helped to conquer, he needed to settle down, and to accept some of the political, economic, and cultural ideals of his sedentary subjects.
—MORRIS ROSSABI
American historian

A Yüan dynasty storage jar showing some of the new, freer artistic designs encouraged by the Mongols. Well aware of the world's admiration for Chinese pottery, Kublai took control of the kilns and monopolized the ceramics trade.

out earth around its roots. When asked why this was so, Cheng replied that the earth had been "stolen by the barbarians."

Kublai was, however, the patron of the greatest Chinese painter of the time, Chao Meng-fu, who eventually became president of the Hanlin Academy, the most prestigious body of scholars in China. Since Chao was a minor member of the Sung imperial family, his service to the court gave considerable weight to Kublai's claims of legitimacy. In addition to painting, Chao served in several administrative posts for Kublai and helped to reform the postal service. But he was severely criticized by many Confucian scholars, even his teacher Ch'ien Hsüan, who felt that Chao had renounced his Chinese heritage and gone over to the barbarians. Feuds like this taught Kublai that the problems of ruling did not end with military victory.

In ruling an empire as large as China, an effective system of good communications was essential. The Mongol army had already developed a corps of messengers who rode from one relay station to another, changing mounts at each post, to deliver military messages. These stations were called *yams*. Riders were able to find food, shelter, and fresh horses at each yam by showing a *paitze*, a metal dish emblematic of Kublai's authority. As more and more territory fell to Kublai, he expanded this system to more than 10,000 yams, keeping some 400 horses in constant readiness. Kublai's couriers, carrying imperial orders and decrees, could now cover 300 miles in a day by changing mounts every 30 miles. Equally important, facilities at the yams were expanded to accommodate traders and travelers. Merchants moving along the Silk Route could halt their day's journey in safety, knowing that detachments of Mongol cavalry now patrolled the trade routes and logged the progress of each caravan. Furthermore, Kublai improved the quality of the routes themselves, laying roads where once there had only been desert paths. Passes were cut through mountains, and rivers were spanned by new bridges.

The responsibilities of Kublai's government were enormous. It had to collect taxes and tribute, allocate money for roads, canals, and other public works, administer China's vast river-based agricultural system, regulate trade, and maintain the Mon-

A simple bowl from the Mongol period. Kublai's artisans were well treated and enjoyed many benefits denied others. The city of Ta-tu grew to contain vast suburbs of craftsmen, merchants, and traders.

gol army. All this required proper written records. At Kublai's court, scribes and secretaries had to record his commands and edicts. Kublai's decrees were recorded first in Mongol, then laboriously translated into Chinese, and then passed on to other imperial bureaucrats and regional governors. But the nomadic Mongols had little experience with the power of the written word. Their own alphabet had been invented only a short time earlier, during the reign of Genghis Khan, and in a traditional society where a man carried all his wealth with him when he moved, there was little need for record keeping.

Kublai recognized that this was a serious problem. Mongol script was based on the written language of the Uighurs of central Asia and did not transcribe the sounds of either the Mongol or the Chinese languages with great precision. Kublai needed a new script that was both accurate and flexible, for he wished to represent the sounds of Chinese names, titles, and offices in his official records. For political reasons, he did not wish to adopt the written language of China. It was pictographic instead of phonetic; its written symbols did not quickly indicate how the words were to be pronounced. It would have taken Kublai's administrators many years to learn to read such a language. That would have made them dependent on the Confucian scribes, whose loyalty was doubtful. Kublai had already decreed that the colloquial, or commonly spoken, form of Chinese would be used for all court records, replacing the classical literary form. This in itself was revolutionary, and it had the effect of undermining the traditional power of the Chinese scholar-bureaucrats. But Kublai felt that even this was not enough, and he had one of the earliest visions of a universal language embracing both the Mongol tongue and all the dialects of Chinese.

Kublai assigned the Tibetan 'Phags-pa lama the task of developing a better and more widely usable script. The 'Phags-pa lama devised a script consisting of 41 letters. Many of the letters were square shaped, leading to the name Square Script, al-

though the official name for the alphabet was 'Phags-pa Script, in honor of its inventor. Kublai was delighted with the new alphabet. He had great expectations for it and ordered it to be used for all official documents.

Although Kublai founded academies for the dissemination of 'Phags-pa Script, the alphabet was never readily adopted. Even Kublai's officials evaded his decree to use the alphabet. 'Phags-pa Script had its widest circulation on coins, paper money, and porcelain but little success in official records and correspondence. Kublai's dream of a universal script was never fulfilled. He had been defeated by the weight of tradition.

There was prosperity under Kublai's reign, and the cities grew rapidly. Larger and wealthier urban populations had more leisure time and the need for more entertainments. With the Great Khan's patronage, theaters flourished. Kublai elevated the status of actors and actresses, and theatrical districts sprang up in all the cities of his empire. Many Confucian scholars, their chances for an official career dashed, turned their literary talents to producing plays.

The plays of this time were a sort of variety entertainment and would not be recognizable to the modern theatergoer as either tragedies or comedies.

Grooms and Horses by three generations of the Chao family. Chao Mengfu, the first to work on this painting, was the greatest Chinese artist to serve Kublai. His theme is a typically Mongol one. Not all Chinese artists, scholars, or poets would willingly serve the Mongols. Many regretted the defeat of the Sung rulers and never overcame their hatred for the northern barbarians.

A silver coin minted in the early years of the Mongol conquest, before Kublai became the Great Khan. It depicts a mounted archer and is inscribed in Persian script, the Mongols having no written language of their own at this time.

Dramatic sketches were interspersed with songs and dances. The plays were supposed to amuse their audiences without seriously interfering in their tea drinking, conversation, and other pleasures. The language of the plays was the colloquial Chinese that Kublai had adopted at court. Use of everyday speech instead of classical language made the plays more accessible to ordinary Chinese. Kublai himself ordered the staging of a number of plays at court and reportedly enjoyed them immensely. Of the 500 or so plays of this period that we know about, 160 scripts have survived. For centuries they were altered to the tastes of each new dynasty, and today they are still performed as "Peking opera."

Kublai's official emphasis on colloquial language encouraged novelists as well as playwrights to produce works about ordinary people instead of imitating classical tales about princes and heroes. Kublai also founded an official government press and granted agricultural land to academies so that they could use the income from the territory to print books. Texts produced during Kublai's reign re-

A bronze coin minted some time after Kublai ascended the throne. It features the "square" lettering of the new system of writing that Kublai tried to introduce in order to give the Mongols their own alphabet.

ceived wide circulation. Chinese classical poetry and the traditional classical essay, the domain of the Confucian scholar, were unappreciated by the court and languished under Kublai's rule.

The Mongol heritage included no traditional or classical forms. There were no rules to follow, and so Kublai allowed his craftsmen and artists great artistic freedom. Under this policy, the output of artistic genius was tremendous and varied. Though they could be cruel masters, the Mongols, because of their need to break the remaining power of the Sung aristocracy, encouraged a more popular culture, and for many Chinese, Kublai's reign was a magnificent renascence, or rebirth, of artistic expression.

Those involved in science and medicine also fared well under Kublai's reign. Perhaps because he himself was afflicted with gout and other ailments, mostly the result of the Mongol diet of rich, fatty foods and vast quantities of koumiss, Kublai established two imperial hospitals to serve his court. He also established an Imperial Academy of Medicine

Two stone figures of Beijing opera actors. Kublai also promoted the dramatic arts, and public performances in theaters and teahouses became all the rage with the growing numbers of merchants, artisans, and court officials who swelled the population of the capital city.

to regulate and supervise the training of physicians and the preparation of medical texts. This helped to raise the standards of medical care and elevated the social status of the physician. Kublai also offered physicians exemptions from corvée labor and taxes. Medicine became an attractive profession for educated Chinese who were unwilling or unable to enter government service.

Scientists and astronomers were also held in high regard. Kublai invited the Persian astronomer Jā-mal al-Dīn to visit his court at Ta-tu. The astrono-

mer brought as gifts diagrams of an armillary sphere, sundials, an astrolabe, and a terrestrial globe. The Chinese astronomer Kuo Shou-ching used the Persian diagrams to construct the instruments at Kublai's court. As a result, the Chinese made many advances in astronomy and mapmaking during this time. Kublai's Astronomical Observatory in Beijing was recently restored and reopened to visitors.

Kublai eliminated many discriminatory practices and raised the social status of the scientific professions, which had not been favored under the Sung. With the abolition of the civil service examination system, the Chinese elite had no means of employment, and many chose to serve in the arts and sciences. Their accomplishments in these fields added to Kublai's image as a true emperor of China, worthy of the Mandate of Heaven.

Borrowing instruments and knowledge from the Persian astronomers, Kublai built his own observatory in Ta-tu. During his reign, a new and more accurate calendar was introduced, and other sciences flourished as well.

8

The Final Days of Kublai

Behind the magnificent facade that Kublai had erected in his capital city, there was internal unrest, and in the later years of his reign this unrest seriously threatened his empire. In 1287 there were rebellions in the outlying regions of Tibet and Manchuria. In Tibet, the close relationship Kublai had established with the 'Phags-pa lama of the Sa-skya sect created unrest among other Buddhist groups who resented his privileged position. When the 'Phags-pa lama died suddenly, Kublai chose the Tibetan ruler's nephew to succeed him. But the selection of a child ruler, raised at Kublai's court, far from the land he was to rule, provoked rebellion. Monasteries were destroyed, and Kublai's troops were attacked. Kublai immediately dispatched his grandson, Temür Bukhe, with a punitive force. Temür Bukhe successfully quashed the rebellion, killing 10,000 men and destroying the monasteries of the dissident Buddhist sects.

The attentions and the honors so lavishly showered upon him by his subjects were unable to keep him, as he had hoped, in eternal spring.
—HENRY and
DANA LEE THOMAS
historians, on the
decline
of Kublai

This European engraving shows a battle between the forces of Kublai and those of Nayan, yet another Mongol challenger for the throne. Based in Manchuria, Nayan allied himself with Khaidu in western Asia, and both accused Kublai of adopting Chinese over Mongolian values.

In Manchuria the rebellion was more serious. Its leader was a distant cousin of Kublai's named Nayan, but behind Nayan was Kublai's old nemesis, Khaidu, the wolf of the steppes, who had continued to harass Kublai's lands all along. Now, just as Khaidu had done earlier, Nayan accused Kublai of betraying his nomadic Mongol heritage and succumbing to China's sedentary civilization. Khaidu and Nayan decided to join forces to coordinate their attack on Kublai.

In 1288, Kublai dispatched his old friend Bayan to hold the forces of Khaidu near Karakorum while the Great Khan himself, realizing the gravity of the situation, personally led his forces against Nayan. Kublai was 72 years old and in poor health when he set off for Manchuria with his troops. He was afflicted by both gout and rheumatism and was no

So serious was the threat from Nayan that Kublai, at the age of 72 and in poor health, personally led his troops into battle. No longer able to ride a horse, he set forth in his famous wooden battle tower supported by four elephants.

longer able to ride a horse. He came to the battlefield on a platform mounted on the backs of four elephants. All the same, his diviners had predicted victory.

When the two armies met, the battle raged from morning to midday before Kublai knew that the promised victory was his. Nayan himself was captured, and Kublai executed him in the traditional manner reserved for Mongol princes of the blood. The rebel prince was rolled tightly in a carpet. The carpet was then placed on the ground, and a division of Kublai's troops galloped across it. Nayan was buried in the carpet so that not a drop of royal Mongol blood would ever touch the ground.

In these last years of his reign, Kublai, having defeated his internal enemies, mounted a series of foreign military expeditions to extend his rule, but most ended disastrously. The largest of these expeditions was directed against Japan. Kublai had repeatedly sent envoys to Japan to establish a relationship with the emperor. But the real power of Japan at this time was in the hands of a shogun, a military governor, named Hōjō Tokimune, who unceremoniously rebuffed Kublai's overtures and even executed his unfortunate envoys, claiming they were spies. Furious at the Japanese refusal to concede his dominion and outraged at the treatment of his envoys, Kublai prepared to launch a naval invasion of Japan.

The Mongols had limited naval battle experience and relied on large contingents of Korean and former Sung troops to provide expertise. Kublai's fleet carried a combined army of more than 140,000 men. In 1284, one contingent of his forces landed on Kyushu, Japan's southernmost main island. The troops intended to battle their way north to rendezvous with other forces, but that summer they were hit by what the Japanese called the *kamikaze*, or "divine wind," a tropical typhoon. The troops retreated to their ships and tried desperately to steer them into the open sea to avoid being driven onto the rocks. But their efforts were futile. The typhoon killed almost half of Kublai's soldiers and destroyed much of his fleet. Many of Kublai's men were washed

A scene from the ill-fated Mongol invasion of Japan, by a Japanese artist. With bows at the ready, the Mongols, beating their war drums, are portrayed as ruthless fighters, merciless to their captives.

up on the shores, where they were slaughtered or taken prisoner by Japanese troops.

To the Japanese, the typhoon was truly a divine wind, a message from the gods that Japan would never fall into enemy hands. The message to Kublai was a bitter one. His prestige was badly bruised, and the psychological edge of terror his army had always held over its opponents was badly shaken. Kublai's invincible army had suffered a severe setback.

The Japanese expedition was only one of Kublai's ill-fated military adventures. He launched a series of invasions against Malaya, Indonesia, and Indochina, hoping to assert his control over the lands bordering southern China, but the Mongol empire had reached the limits of the possible. Where the enemy's army could not stop him, the heat and humidity of the jungle proved too much for his troops. Thousands dropped from tropical diseases or sheer exhaustion. The core of the Mongol army, the unstoppable cavalry, was useless in the mountainous, forested terrain of Southeast Asia. There were some victories, but control of these tributary states, especially in Indochina, was costly and uncertain.

Kublai's military expedition against Java in 1293, a year before his death, was another disaster. When Kublai's envoy arrived at the court of Java to demand the submission of King Kertanagara, the king ordered his guards to brand the messenger's face. King Kertanagara sought to control spice production in the Moluccas and to have the Javanese serve as middlemen in the spice trade. He feared that Kublai wished to take control of this lucrative commerce.

Kublai assembled a multinational force consisting of 20,000 men in 1,000 boats, and he provided them with a year's store of grain. King Kertanagara split his army and dispatched two large forces to the points where he assumed Kublai's invading fleet would land. But spreading his forces had left him vulnerable to a rebellious Javanese faction, which attacked Kertanagara's troops and killed the king. Prince Vijaya, his son-in-law, inherited the throne and offered his submission to the Khan's forces in return for their help in crushing the rebels who had killed his father-in-law. Kublai's generals willingly accepted the proposal and defeated the Javanese rebels easily.

Vijaya now asked for 200 unarmed men to escort him to the town where he would officially submit to Kublai. But Kublai's generals had not foreseen Vijaya's duplicity. The prince's troops ambushed his Mongol escorts and quietly concentrated their forces to surround the generals waiting for his surrender. Kublai's generals barely escaped with their life, losing thousands of troops in their battle to reach their ships.

Kublai's failed military adventures caused tremendous damage to his prestige and strained the resources of his empire. Although the Mongol forces brought back incense, perfumes, rhinoceros horns, and ivory from their invasion of Java, the value of these goods could not compensate for the losses in

Two boatloads of samurai warriors put to sea to "mop up" the floundering Mongol fleet. These foreign military adventures bankrupted Kublai's court and forced him to print paper money to pay the costs of his armies.

men and the expense of campaigning. The real wealth of China at this time was in its agriculture. In spite of Kublai's improvements, the Chinese peasants were heavily oppressed by local landlords and Mongol overseers and the first to suffer from floods and droughts. The productivity of farms was low by modern standards, and the few luxury goods brought back from foreign wars could not feed armies. Kublai's magnificent courts at Ta-tu and Shang-tu, with their entertainments, feasts, and hunts, also entailed great expense. His patronage of the arts further drained his resources. Great public works, such as his extension of the Grand Canal and the new postal system, made heavy demands on his treasury. Severe revenue problems began to plague him.

To add to all his problems, Kublai's finance minister, a Muslim from central Asia named Ahmad, proved to be dishonest. Ahmad had originally been recommended to Kublai by Chabi in what was certainly her greatest failure as Kublai's adviser. As Ahmad's power grew, so did his excesses, both personal and financial. He enriched himself considerably by abusing his position. He appointed relatives and friends to positions for which they were unqualified. He speculated on fluctuations in the prices of goods to enrich himself. Marco Polo relates: "Whenever he learnt that someone had a good-looking daughter, he would send his ruffians to the girl's father, and they would say: 'What is your ambition? Well then, how about this daughter of yours?' " And so a man might purchase his office by corrupting his children, knowing that the Khan himself would agree to Ahmad's choice.

Kublai's Confucian ministers repeatedly objected to Ahmad's policies and to their effect on the Chinese population, but Kublai did not completely trust the Confucians. Ahmad exploited Kublai's suspicions, falsely accused the ministers who opposed him, and had them executed.

On an April evening in 1282, when Kublai was in Shang-tu, a group of Confucians lured Ahmad outside his house and assassinated him. When Kublai returned to Ta-tu, he executed the conspirators. His

The Emperor was so fond of [Ahmad] that he gave him a completely free hand. It seems, as was learnt after his death, that this Ahmad used to bewitch the Emperor by his black arts to such purpose that he won a ready hearing and acceptance for everything he said; and so he was free to do whatever he chose.

—MARCO POLO
Venetian traveler

remaining advisers, however, finally persuaded him of Ahmad's treachery and corruption. A costly jewel that had been presented to Kublai himself was found in Ahmad's house. Kublai had Ahmad's body exhumed and hung in a bazaar at Ta-tu. Then he had it placed on the ground and ordered carts driven over the head. His dogs then attacked the corpse. Several of Ahmad's sons were executed, and his property was confiscated. Most of the officials that Ahmad had appointed were dismissed.

Financial worries were overshadowed in 1281 by the tragic death of Chabi. Kublai was left heartbroken by the loss of his beloved wife. He erected a

Campaigns in the jungles of Southeast Asia proved equally disastrous for Kublai. Heat and disease took an enormous toll on his troops, and he was never able to control these client states.

memorial tablet to her in his temple and offered sacrifices and prayers to her spirit. But he sank into a deep depression, withdrawing from the court and seeing fewer and fewer of his advisers. He began to eat and drink to excess, and his health began to decline dangerously. Gout caused his feet to become too painful for much walking. Special shoes of fish skin imported from Korea were made in Kublai's workshops to alleviate his discomfort. Rheumatism made his bones ache, and his growing obesity exacerbated these problems.

Shortly before her death, when Chabi realized that her health was failing, she had looked among Kublai's minor wives for her own eventual successor. She searched for a traditional Mongol wife who would be both personally and politically assertive and finally chose a distant relative of her own named Nambi. In Kublai's old age, Nambi increasingly made political decisions for him as he began to with-

Kublai and Chabi camped on the steppes. Unlike so many other royal marriages, this was a relationship based on love. When Chabi died, Kublai became depressed and withdrew from the responsibilities of government. He actually abdicated in favor of his son two years before his own death.

draw from active government. Memorials and reports to the throne were presented directly to Nambi, and she issued edicts in Kublai's name as his health declined.

Kublai had abandoned the Mongol khuriltai, the council of nobles who elected the ruler, in favor of the Chinese method, by which the emperor himself designated his successor. He had chosen Chabi's son Chen-chin as his heir. As the future emperor of China, Chen-chin had been carefully groomed to assume the duties of the throne. He had studied the Confucian classics and Chinese history as well as military tactics and warfare. But in 1285, only four years after his mother's demise, Chen-chin died. He was in his forties, and his death further deepened Kublai's depression. Kublai now designated his grandson Temür as his heir. Shattered in body and spirit, Kublai stepped down from the throne in 1294, and Temür became emperor.

The remote grasslands of Mongolia, where Kublai and all the Great Khans of his line were taken for burial. Kublai died in 1294, and within a short time the empire he had built through a lifetime of conquests was divided and swept into history.

Kublai had chosen well. Temür was a prudent leader, but all the damage done by years of foreign wars, extravagant expenses at court, and Ahmad's financial mismanagement could not be undone. The paper money that Kublai had introduced, made of the bark of mulberry leaves, depreciated, and inflation followed. With rising prices came greater impoverishment of the lower classes, and in 1368 a peasant rebellion in southern China toppled the dynasty Kublai had founded. The Yüan dynasty had lasted less than 100 years and was quickly swallowed up by the new Ming dynasty, which would last for more than 250 years.

In 1294, Kublai died in his palace at Ta-tu. A vast and solemn caravan conveyed his body to the Kentey Mountains, where his grandfather, Genghis Khan, had been buried 70 years before. Like the tomb of Genghis, the precise site of Kublai's burial was not recorded and remains unknown. Once the underground vault was sealed, Kublai's troops passed in review one last time. The mounted soldiers of the Mongol army galloped across the plain, obliterating all traces of Kublai's tomb from the face of the earth. The ruler of one of the greatest empires that the world has known still lies undisturbed somewhere on the harsh steppes of the Mongolian Plateau.

Further Reading

Boyle, J. A. *The Successors of Genghis Khan.* New York: Columbia University Press, 1971.

Chambers, John. *The Devil's Horsemen.* London: Weidenfeld and Nicolson, 1979.

Curtin, Jeremiah. *The Mongols: A History.* Boston: Little, Brown, 1908.

Dardess, John W. *Conquerors and Confucians.* New York: Columbia University Press, 1973.

Eberhard, Wolfram. *A History of China.* Berkeley: University of California Press, 1977.

Fairbank, John F., Edwin O. Reischauer, and Albert M. Craig. *East Asia: Tradition and Transformation.* Boston: Houghton Mifflin, 1973.

Grousset, René. *The Rise and Splendour of the Chinese Empire.* Berkeley: University of California Press, 1952.

Halperin, Charles J. *Russia and the Golden Horde.* Bloomington: Indiana University Press, 1985.

Humphrey, Judy. *Genghis Khan.* New York: Chelsea House, 1987.

Olschki, Leonardo. *Marco Polo's Asia.* Berkeley: University of California Press, 1960.

Phillips, J. R. S. *The Medieval Expansion of Europe.* New York: Oxford University Press, 1988.

Polo, Marco. *The Travels.* Translated by Ronald Latham. Middlesex, England: Penguin, 1958.

Prawdin, Michael. *The Mongol Empire: Its Rise and Legacy.* New York: Macmillan, 1940.

Rossabi, Morris. *Khubilai Khan, His Life and Times.* Berkeley: University of California Press, 1983.

Saunders, J. J. *History of the Mongols: Based on Eastern and Western Accounts of the 13th and 14th Centuries.* Berkeley: University of California Press, 1972.

Waley, Arthur. *Secret History of the Mongols.* New York: Barnes and Noble, 1964.

Chronology

Sept. 23, 1215	Born Kublai, Son of Sorghaghtani Beki and Tolui
1224	Initiated at Great Hunt by grandfather Genghis Khan
1227	Genghis Khan dies
1229	Genghis's son Ögödei is named Khan of Khans
1236	Kublai assumes appanage of Hsing-chou in northern China
1239	Marries second wife, Chabi
1241	Ögödei dies
1251	Mangu is elected Great Khan
1259	Mangu dies
1260	*Khuriltai* held in northern China elects Kublai Great Khan; Arigböge is unofficially proclaimed Great Khan by his supporters; Kublai establishes capital at Beijing; charitable works for poor and sick is established
1264	Arigböge concedes defeat to Kublai
1267	Khaidu establishes stronghold in Central Asia; Kublai establishes new capital called Chung-tu
1271	Declares himself emperor of Chinese Yüan dynasty
1273	Fall of Fan-ch'eng and Hsiang-yang
1276	Sung capital of Hangchow capitulates
1279	Kublai crushes remnants of the Sung dynasty and becomes ruler of all China; Chabi dies
1281	Kamikaze typhoon disperses Kublai's armada in Japan
1292	Kublai's armada attacks Java
1294	Kublai's grandson, Temür, is chosen to succeed him as emperor of China
Feb. 18, 1294	Kublai dies

Index

Kim Dramer is a Ph.D. candidate in East Asian art history at Columbia University. She has traveled extensively in China, and her articles on Chinese art and culture have appeared in numerous publications, including the *New York Times*, the New York *Daily News*, *Ovation* magazine, and *Opera Canada* magazine.

Arthur M. Schlesinger, jr., taught history at Harvard for many years and is currently Albert Schweitzer Professor of the Humanities at City University of New York. He is the author of numerous highly praised works in American history and has twice been awarded the Pulitzer Prize. He served in the White House as special assistant to Presidents Kennedy and Johnson.

PICTURE CREDITS